An Introduction to Distributed Data Processing

an introduction to

PBI
A PETROCELLI BOOK
new york / princeton

Distributed Data Processing

HARRY KATZAN, Jr.
Pratt Institute

Printed in the United States

1 2 3 4 5 6 7 8 9 10

Library of Congress Cataloging in Publication Data

Katzan, Harry.
An Introduction to distributed data processing.

Bibliography: p.
Includes index.
1. Electronic data processing—Distributed processing. I. Title.
QA76.9.D5K37 001.6'4 78-27323
ISBN 0-89433-061-6

. . . there is nothing more difficult to take in hand, more perilous to conduct, or more uncertain in its success, than to take the lead in the introduction of a new order of things. Because the innovator has for enemies all those who have done well under the old conditions, and lukewarm defenders in those who may do well under the new. This coolness arises partly from fear of the opponents, who have the laws on their side, and partly from the incredulity of men, who do not readily believe in new things until they have a long experience of them.

Machiavelli
The Prince
1513

contents

Appendices

preface

Two functions that are fundamental to organized society are communication and dispersion. Communication provides a means for information to be accumulated, and dispersion permits effective and efficient use of resources.

Communication and dispersion also provide the basis for a major technological advance in the computer field known as Distributed Data Processing or DDP for short. The move to DDP has been a quiet revolution since it supports the information dynamics of organizations and proposes to match computer facilities with organizational structure. The key issue is centralization versus decentralization and the move to DDP offers five general benefits: reliability, responsiveness, incremental growth, correspondence to organizational patterns, and resource sharing. Distributed data processing is more than a product of advanced technology in micro- and minicomputers, communications, and data base systems; it represents an evolving confidence in management's ability to control the computer rather than have the computer control them.

Distributed data processing is a new technology and exists as a plethora of conflicting concepts and confusing terminology. The objective of this book is to summarize the key concepts of distributed data processing from an introductory point of view. Distributed data processing has been described as a "concept in search of a definition." The risk of criticism for "trodding where no one else has dared trod" is obvious.

The book is introductory and consists of three parts and three appendices. Part One, Management Overview, covers basic concepts, considerations in a distributed environment, and a management philosophy of distributed systems. Part Two, Data Communications Concepts, covers introduction to data communications, computer networks, network functions and components, and network procedures. Part Three, Distributed Systems Concepts, covers distributed data processing systems and distributed data base systems. The appendices include methods for determining the effectiveness of distributed systems, a guide to abbreviations and acronyms in data communications and a guide to data communications buzzwords.

The book is intended for executives, managers, analysts, and programmers. The subject matter can be used as an overview of distributed systems concepts or as a study of some of its technical characteristics.

It is a pleasure to acknowledge the insight and cooperation of the publisher, O.R. Petrocelli, for the foresight to publish a book on the ground-breaking subject of Distributed Data Processing and the contribution of Mary Ann Vezzosi in expertly managing the complex task of producing the book. My wife Margaret assisted with the manuscript preparation and was an excellent partner during the entire project.

part one

Management Overview

1

Basic Concepts

One of the most significant items of terminology to surface in the broad technological area of computers and data processing is "Distributed Data Processing," or DDP for short. Familiar aliases are distributed systems, distributed processing, and distributed networks. Literally hundreds of articles have been published in the popular and trade media, and most of those are minimally definitive and primarily entertaining. Computer vendors, large and small, commonly use the acronym DDP as an "attention grabber" for the marketing of conventional computer equipment. Some writers have termed distributed data processing as a concept in search of a definition. In spite of the situation, DDP appears to satisfy an actual need in modern society, as we know it, and is considerably more than simply the "germ of a good idea."

Need for Communication and Dispersion

Without the ability to communicate, we would be forced to obtain "everything" for ourselves. This statement is intended to be interpreted in the widest possible sense to include the activities of individuals, groups, societies, and systems. Communication provides the means for the accumulation of information, the centralization of inherent knowledge, and the specialization of individualized and organized activity.

Dispersion permits effective and efficient use of available resources. Effectiveness and efficiency are achieved through local management and economic control over the dispersal of resources and the application of specialized knowledge. In any complex system, no one person has complete knowledge of each functional capability, but some people at least have a working knowledge of each.

Communication and dispersion go hand in hand, since communication permits the existence of specialized activity that gives us the potential for technological or economic gains inherent in dispersion that would not be possible otherwise.

Dispersion of Computing Facilities

Computing facilities are dispersed when there is a need for local processing under local control. This method of distribution enables local management to be more effective and yet be responsive to the needs of central management. The key words here are distribution, local management, and central management, because they are the three necessary ingredients in a distributed system.

A *distributed system* is one in which computers—usually minicomputers—are located in sites that are remote from a central computing facility and those computers possess the physical attributes that permit them to interact with the central facility and possibly with each other. The objective of distributed computing is to process information where it is most effective to satisfy operational, economic, or geographic conditions.

Characteristics of a Distributed System

A local computer in a distributed system has the general characteristics of a small stand-alone data processing system. The computer is under the operational control of local management and is normally required to do the processing of a given set of applications, such as accounts receivable, accounts payable, and inventory control, for its host facility. In a centralized system, the same set of applications would be processed by the central facility for the remote installation. Thus, the control of a distributed application and the processing of the application are distributed to the remote location—hence the inherent terminology of distributed system and distributed computing.

With a distributed system, local management is responsible for maintaining a given set of computer applications in a production mode and for performing traditional installation management tasks.

A distributed system is additionally characterized by a local data store, which may take the form of a set of files or a data base, depending upon the local processing that is required. In fact, local storage may be increased to the extent that the dispersed minicomputer may begin to approach the capacity of a medium-scale system.

A final characteristic is that of telecommunications facilities that tie the local computer to the central facility. While a strong case can be made for defining a distributed system without telecommunications facilities and using other means of communication, the concept loses most of its operational flavor without telecommunications. However, distributed computing does not automatically imply an on-line demand-response type of operation such that a considerable amount of latitude is given in the manner of using telecommunications facilities. For example, communications in a distributed system between a central and local computer may take place in off hours using relatively unsophisticated telecommunications facilities.

Operation of a Distributed System

The essence of a distributed system is to perform some data processing tasks at the points of user activity, while permitting other tasks to be transmitted to a centralized facility for processing. The concept necessarily includes the transferring between adjacent systems of informational resources, which may take the form of data base structures or computed results. Programs may also be transferred between locations in a distributed system.

In a distributed computing environment, source data entry takes place at the local site and is received at one of the dispersed computers—either through a hardwire connection or through local telecommunications facilities. Thus, source data is maintained at its point of origin, which most EDP auditors feel is the most desirable situation. Whenever possible, processing is performed locally and summary information is communicated from the dispersed computer to the central facility for review and for incorporation into central files or into the centralized data base. In cases for which source data must be processed at the central computer facility, the dispersed computer would be used to verify and store the data locally and then transmit it via telecommunications facilities to the central computer facility for processing. Computed results would then be transmitted from the central computer facility to the local computer system for printing and possibly local storage.

In a data base environment, a local data base is maintained at the dispersed computer site as though it were a stand-alone self-contained system. Then on a periodic basis, data is transferred via telecommunications facilities between the centralized data base and the dispersed data base to maintain each in a specified level of synchronism.

Typical Distributed Applications

Two typical examples of distributed data processing applications are payroll and inventory control. Both applications are conceptually straightforward but involve operational situations wherein two levels of control are needed: centralized and local.

In the distributed payroll application, payroll data is collected locally and stored in the local data base or as local files. The raw data necessary for payroll processing is then transmitted to the central location. In the centralized computing facility, the payroll is computed and the information from which checks can be printed is generated as files—one file for each dispersed location. Paycheck data is then transmitted to the dispersed computer installations and stored. Subsequently, the checks are printed locally.

In the distributed inventory control application, sales transactions are handled at the dispersed location while purchasing and management control are handled at the central location. A common example of a distributed system of this type would be a retail chain of stores that use intelligent terminals for sales transactions with a minicomputer, located somewhere in the store for record keeping and inventory management. Then on a periodic basis, the dispersed minicomputers transmit summary data to a central computer facility, wherein the purchasing function has been consolidated to obtain large quantity discounts. The combination of the local minicomputer together with the intelligent terminal—i.e., a computerized cash register—also provides a means of achieving dynamic inventory control.

Management of a Distributed System

Local control over a dispersed computing facility also involves management of that facility with all of the problems inherent therein. There are obvious benefits to local control since management responsibility usually determines accountability.

In a distributed data processing environment, the first level of management responsibility is the justification and acquisition of computer equipment, including data entry devices, mainframes, peripheral and mass storage devices, and communications equipment. In most cases, a staff service from the central facility will be available for assistance in this regard; however, local processing requirements may require a certain amount of sophistication in configuration management at the local level.

The second level of management responsibility involves people, and it is sufficient to mention that the following areas must be covered: data entry, operational control, systems people and programmers, source data control, and local DP management. Other than traditional functions, areas necessarily covered by the systems people and programmers include communications protocols between dispersed systems, data security, and data base management.

Another level of management responsibility concerns the physical installation and computer security. With the multiplicity of programs and files inherent in a distributed system, the opportunity for catastrophe, fraud, and embezzlement are compounded and a comprehensive program of risk assessment is necessary.

A final area of management responsibility is the determination of the specific kinds of data processing that are performed and their cost justification. A distributed system is a powerful resource, and an overindulgence in data processing can easily lead to decreased job satisfaction and anxiety among non-DP workers whose tasks require adherence to time deadlines related to the computer requirements.

Overall, the effect of data processing technology is that there is a tendency to shift power to that department and executive that has the computer.

Problems in a Distributed System Environment

Any new technology is not without its problems and distributed data processing is certainly no exception. In addition to the requirements, stated above, for effective utilization and management of a dispersed computer system, three major problems normally encountered with a distributed system involve the data base, communications interface, and the need for operational integrity, implied above.

The motivation for developing a data base in the first place is to reduce data redundancy, and the notion of having a data base dispersed to different locations would seem to be contrary to the basic philosophy. The key problem here is replication of portions of the data base and this can cause problems of currency, control, and security.

In some distributed systems, the dispersed computer systems will be of the same brand and model—possibly selected by a central service staff in association with local management. Due to the wide variations in needs of remote locations, however, it is likely that a major problem will be the interfacing and interaction of a dispersed minicomputer with another minicomputer or the central computer facility. In most cases this kind of problem will involve the design and development of communications protocols.

Problems involving operational integrity can hardly be minimized. Because of the relatively high number of people interacting with the distributed system from dispersed locations, considerations of security, integrity, and control must simply be more comprehensive and more stringent than what would be normally required in a nondistributed system.

Programs in a Distributed System

The biggest expense in modern data processing involves application programs and this category would be expected to increase because of different needs caused by the diversity of dispersed locations. Some application programs, such as payroll check printing programs, can be prepared by a central service staff and distributed accordingly. When different computer systems are involved, then standard conversion methods can be applied, provided that the programs are written in a common language such as COBOL or RPG.

In some cases, programs developed for the central computing facility will have to be modified for use at a dispersed location. This process can also be simplified if common programming languages are used.

Programs developed specially for a dispersed computer system should also be written in a common programming language—regardless of the temptation for programming in assembler language. In fact, the motivation for programming in assembler language may be substantial, especially when a smaller and less costly dispersed computer system would be required because of it. Nevertheless, the capability of exchanging programs between dispersed locations is important from the point of view of economics and of software reliability.

Solving the Total Problem

With the current impetus toward computer communication networks, one would tacitly assume that a move to distributed data processing would simply be a move in the same direction. Technically, this is probably true. However, distributed data processing affects organizational structures, personnel, and management philosophy in addition to being a part of the whole human communications picture. Unlike many other types of systems, a distributed system should be modeled in order to achieve a workable and an effective system. Therefore, it is particularly important that the prospective manager or administrator in a distributed systems environment solves the "total distributed problem." The remainder of the book is organized with that purpose in mind.

Summary

Communication and dispersion are fundamental to organized society since communication provides the means for information to be accumulated and dispersion permits effective and efficient use of resources. Computing facilities are dispersed when there is a need for local processing under local control, and through the use of telecommunications facilities, local computers can communicate with each other and with a central computing facility. This is *distributed data processing* in which information is processed where it is most effective to satisfy operational, economic, or geographic conditions.

A local computer in a distributed system can be used as a small standalone data processing system so that some data processing tasks can be performed locally while others are transmitted to a centralized facility for processing. Typical distributed data processing applications are payroll and inventory control which characteristically required processing activity at both the central and local computing facilities.

Management tasks in a distributed environment typically involve computer acquisition, people management, the physical facility, and computer applications. Management problems usually involve the data base, communications interface, and computer and data security.

2

Considerations in a Distributed Environment

Any organization that has moved or is contemplating a move in the direction of a distributed system recognizes that the existence of dispersed computing facilities has slowly evolved. Through the years, independent parts of the organization acquired computers and unless explicit control existed over expenditures of this type, it is likely that the hardware is incompatible and possibly inappropriate to local needs. For example, one department could be overloaded and be buying time outside of the organization, while another department could be underloaded with the computer idle a good percentage of the time. A scientific computer could possibly be being used for data processing applications, while highly paid engineering personnel are "banging out" computations on hand calculators for applications better placed on a general-purpose computer. In other cases, a set of intelligent terminals could possibly be linked to a minicomputer for an application such as price or inventory control with no connection to a central facility. This chapter is concerned with determining what constitutes a distributed system.

Distributed Systems in Perspective

"Many users today view the new 'distributed' concepts as a means of fitting computer resources (solutions) to their organizational needs (problems) as opposed to the previously customary fitting of the problem to the solution."[1] This quotation appears to be the start of another vicious attack on

[1]Becker, H.B., "Let's Put Information Networks into Perspective," *Datamation* (March 1978): 81.

data processing management, but it is not. In fact, it will be very amazing if future distributed data processing management can do as well as their predecessors did in a centralized environment.

Nevertheless, it is well for the distributed systems manager to be aware of at least one opinion, right or wrong, of the current involvement in large centralized computer facilities:

> This evolutionary growth, fostered initially by the manager's neglect, has resulted in internal cost increases, which has lead to product cost increases and contributed to our inflationary economy. . . . In many organizations the computer manufacturer and the data processing professionals have promoted a kind of conspiracy that perpetuates large central computer facilities, permanent positions in data processing, and spiraling costs. The computer manufacturer literally monopolizes, restricts, and dramatically affects internal decision making in many American organizations today by promoting evolutionary increases in data processing expenditures and propagating a fear of change. . . .[2]

While the above quotation may in fact be true, it is this author's opinion that it is not generally representative of actual practice. In fact, it should be regarded as a tribute to the stability of modern data processing management that they stayed as long with centralized facilities as they did. There was and still remains a temptation to "jump on the distributed bandwagon" to ease local management's pressure for acquiring processing capability and to achieve "quick and dirty" cost reductions.

[2]Breslin, J. and C.B. Tashenberg, *Distributed Processing Systems: End of the Mainframe Era?* (New York: AMACOM, 1978), p. 1.

However, it is genuinely felt that the situation is a technical one. It was impossible to disperse data processing until the technologies for communications, minicomputers, intelligent terminals, and data bases were proved out in a business environment. This has been achieved in the past few years and as a direct result, there currently is a high level of interest in distributed systems.

Distributed Systems Identification

"A *distributed system* has been defined as one in which there are several autonomous but interacting processors and/or data stores at different geographical locations."[3] However, the physical distribution of hardware without dispersing the processing function does not constitute a distributed system.

A key property in a distributed system is *anonymity,* which should be interpreted to mean that local computer systems can operate autonomously without direct supervision of a central computer facility or without "permission" of a master computer system. Obviously, operational policies must be available for governing the operation of distributed systems. This subject is covered later.

A remote work station or intelligent terminal programmed to perform routine editing or error correction without a significant amount of file activity is not generally considered to be a distributed computer. However,

[3]Down, P.J. and F.E. Taylor, *Why Distributed Computing?* (Manchester, England: NCC Publications, 1976), p. 6.

a distributed computer may be used in part as a remote job entry/output work station since it possesses all of the necessary hardware facilities.

The NCC report[4] distinguishes between distributed systems and distributed processors. A collection of independent but physically adjacent processors connected by cable is termed a *distributed processor*. A distributed processor may take the form of a set of processors that perform the same function, as in the SOLOMON and ILLIAC IV computers, or different functions, such as communications, arithmetic and logic, input/output control and data base processing. Using the NCC definition, a distributed processor is not geographically dispersed and does not classify as a distributed system. However, the key point here is how tightly coupled the processors are. Clearly, two computer systems that can interchange programs and data via telecommunications facilities and satisfy the property of anonymity should be classed as a distributed system, even though they may be located in close proximity to each other. On the other hand, two computer systems servicing the same job queue via a shared disk unit, two central processors sharing main storage for load leveling, or a primary and a backup system operating in tandem for increased reliability would not be regarded as a distributed system.

The NCC report also distinguishes between a network system and a distributed system. In a network system, a task is transported to a site of optimum effectiveness, not necessarily the host site, whereas in a distributed system, the objective is to process as much of the work as is feasible at the dispersed location. The NCC report summarized the situa-

[4]Ibid., p. 7.

tion well: "Networking takes the job to the processing resource; distribution takes the processing resource to the user."[5]

Snapshot of Reality—Trends in Distributed Systems

It is obvious from the preceding discussion that the definition of a distributed system is more nebulous than we would like it to be. This is partly the case because we have taken a snapshot of reality. Another approach to this elusive subject is suggested by John Kirkley: "Instead of asking 'What is it?', it's more productive to ask 'What does it allow me to do?' "[6]

A partial answer to the second question is given by Liebowitz and Carson as follows:

> To some, a distributed system is a collection of multiple computers or processing elements working closely together in the solution of a single problem. . . .
>
> To other users, a distributed system is a set of intelligent terminals located at the point of use to give local organizational elements more responsive computer support. . . .
>
> To yet another set of users, distributed systems may mean collections of geographically dispersed, independent computing centers linked together to allow the sharing of software and hardware resources. . . .
>
> To some, distributed processing means the use of small computers to off-load

[5]Ibid.
[6]Kirkley, J.L., "Happiness Is Distributed Processing," *Datamation* (March 1978): 79.

> supporting functions from large mainframes, to extend the life of the mainframe. . . .
>
> The common thread linking the different types of distributed systems is the use of multiple cooperating computing elements to perform jobs that were heretofore performed on large computers or not performed at all.[7]

Even though this quotation reflects the current confusion over terminology, it does indicate some of the functions inherent in a distributed system.

It is important that some of the reasons and benefits of distributed systems be identified. One of the major reasons that many organizations originally moved to large centralized computer facilities was to realize the economy of scale inherent in large computers. The development of microprocessor and minicomputer technology, however, has reversed the trend so that, currently, economy of scale can be obtained through a collection of small computers. Another benefit of distributed systems that is frequently not recognized is that local computing has a tendency to reduce the volume of data transmitted over telecommunications facilities, which can usually be equated to lower communications costs. In general, five advantages of dispersed computer systems can be listed: reliability, responsiveness, incremental growth, correspondence to organizational patterns, and resource sharing.[8]

Reliability refers to the capability of adding individual components, such as central processing units, storage units, etc., to increase system

[7]Liebowitz, B.H. and J.H. Carson, *Distributed Processing Tutorial* (New York: IEEE, 1977), p. 1–1.

[8]Ibid., p. 1–2.

availability without requiring that an entire system be replicated. Software that is less complex than in large centralized systems can be used with the notion that the same software can be used in several dispersed locations.

Responsiveness refers to the fact that a local computer system can be managed in such a way that it can more directly satisfy the needs of local organizational management than one located in a central facility and intended to satisfy the needs of the total organization.

The option for *incremental growth* relates to the total distributed system and refers to the manner in which the system is enhanced to satisfy the needs of an increased work load. In a centralized facility, an increased work load usually involves a major equipment purchase, whereas in a distributed system, the capacity of local computer centers can be increased with off-loading of excess data processing, as required. Thus, from the standpoint of the total distributed system, equipment purchases tend to be relatively minor increments in capacity.

Through the nature of business products or other organizational activity, many organizations employ a decentralized structure with corresponding policies and operational procedures. In many cases, the move to centralized data processing has required that adjustments be made to policies and operational procedures with diverse effects on organizational activity, not necessarily directly related to data processing. Through the use of a distributed system, data processing has a closer *correspondence to organizational pattern.* However, a distributed system permits top management "to have their cake and eat it too," since it can be used to combine the benefits of centralized data processing and a decentralized organizational structure.

Resource sharing refers to the inherent economic benefit of a distributed system through the combined use of personnel, programs, data, and computing facilities. Staff services, programs, and data can be developed on an organizationwide basis and distributed to the dispersed facilities. Moreover, each facility can have a "charter" for certain key processing capabilities, so that expensive facilities need not be replicated throughout the system.

Another benefit of a distributed system is that it permits a certain degree of experimentation with new concepts and facilities at a single site, thereby reducing the risk normally associated with systems enhancements.

Elements of a Distributed System

Enslow identifies four physical elements in a distributed system:

1. Hardware or processing logic,
2. Data,
3. The computer processing, and
4. Control, such as the operating system[9]

It necessarily follows that the degree to which a system is distributed is dependent upon the physical distribution of the four elements and the conditions under which they interact.

The most basic ingredient in a distributed system is at least two assigna-

[9]Enslow, P.H., Jr., "What Is a 'Distributed' Data Processing System?" *Computer* 11: 1 (January, 1978): 13.

ble sets of processing facilities that are dispersed as covered above. Associated with the dispersed processing facilities is the existence of dispersed processing. Although dispersed processing may generally be taken for granted, it is important to recognize that the processing capability in a dispersed computer system is frequently not utilized as such. Many intelligent terminals are used as though they were "dumb" terminals, and many small business computers are used as remote job entry work stations.

The physical dispersion of processing facilities must also be accompanied by a method of intercommunication, wherein both parties cooperate in data transfer operations. The operating conventions governing a data transfer operation via telecommunications facilities is referred to as a *communications protocol.*

In a distributed environment, data is classed as static or dynamic. The term *static* refers to distributed files or data bases. The term *dynamic* refers to message data. The role of static data in a distributed environment is one of the least well defined of the elements in a distributed system at this time, and many researchers feel that we will experience distributed files long before we see distributed data bases.

The subject of *control* pertains to the existence of a high-level operating system designed to manage the allocation and utilization of distributed system resources in an efficient and effective manner. Although network operating systems have been designed and developed, the notion of a distributed operating system remains a research topic at this time. The objective of a distributed operating system appears to promote system transparency of resources so as to approximate the function of a network system. Moreover, the notion of a central avenue of control, as compared to independent cooperating systems, also violates the principle of anonymity, mentioned above.

The three elements of degree of hardware decentralization, degree of control decentralization, and degree of data base decentralization are used by Enslow[10] as dimensions characterizing the degree of decentralization in a system. The result of this manner of defining a distributed system is summarized in Figure 2.1, which establishes an allowable region for distributed data processing systems.

Summary

A distributed system can be properly viewed as a means of fitting computer resources to organizational needs—especially when the organizational structure is decentralized. With the evolution and establishment of relevant technology for communications, minicomputers, and intelligent terminals, distributed computing represents an idea whose time has arrived. There is currently a high level of interest in the subject.

A key property of a distributed system is anonymity, which means that local computer facilities have the capability of operating autonomously. Distributed data processing should be distinguished from distributed processors and network systems, which represent different concepts. Through microcomputer and minicomputer technology, the advantages of economy of scale have been changed from large centralized facilities to small decentralized facilities.

[10]Ibid., pp. 17–19.

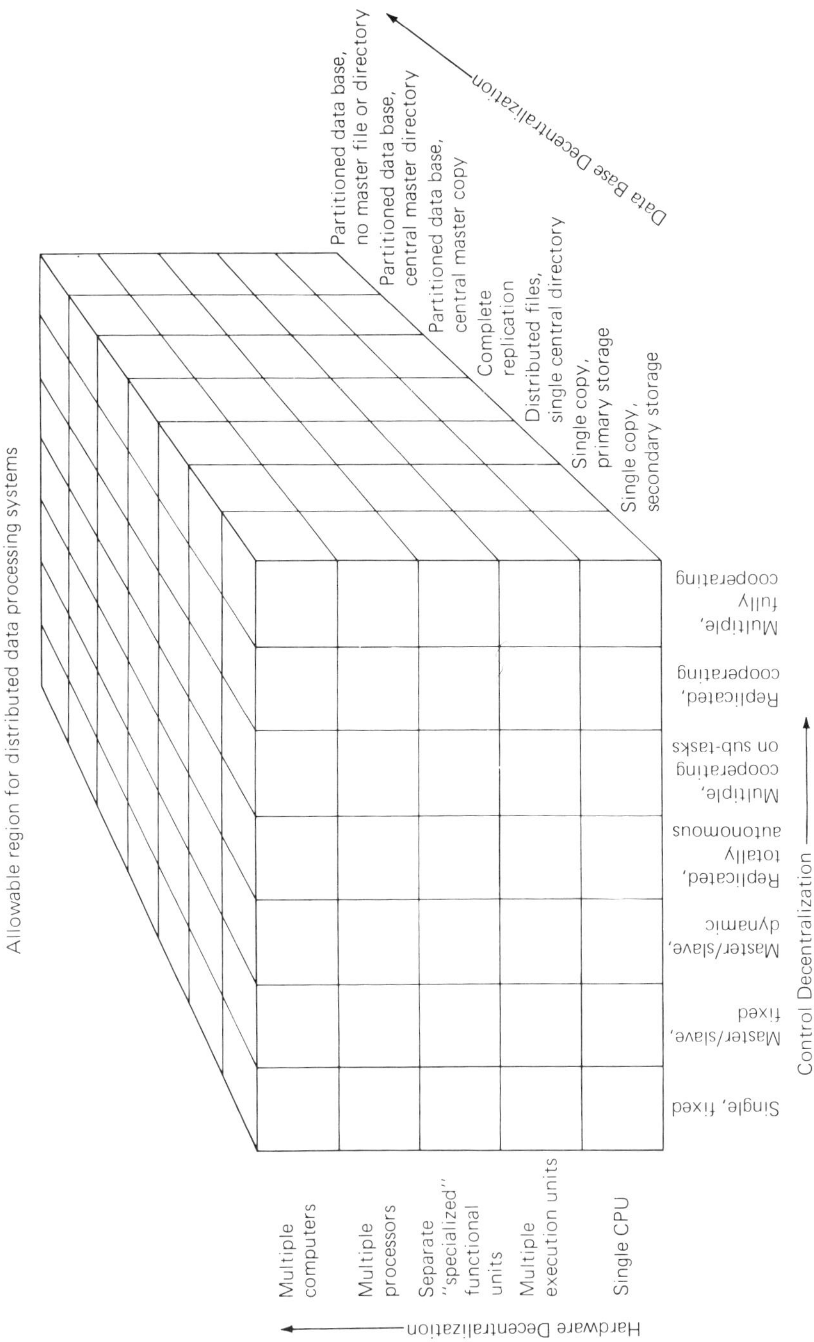

Figure 2.1: Dimensions characterizing the degree of decentralization in a system (Reprinted, with permission, from "What is a 'Distributed' Data Processing System?" by P.H. Enslow, Jr. in Computer, *January 1978.*

Five general benefits of dispersed computer systems are reliability, responsiveness, incremental growth, correspondence to organizational patterns, and resource sharing. The four essential elements of a distributed system are hardware or processing logic, data, computer processing, and control. The degree of decentralization in a computer system is a function of three elements: the degree of hardware decentralization, the degree of control decentralization, and the degree of data base decentralization.

3

Toward a Management Philosophy of Distributed Systems

Clearly, the notion of a distributed system has surfaced as a technical concern ameliorated by noteworthy successes in communication networks and minicomputer technology. There is no theory of distributed systems so that the subject is a pragmatic one closely related to traditional issues in organizational management. While the implementation of a distributed system may be correctly regarded as a technical problem, the organizational impact of a distributed system may be substantial so as to affect day-to-day operations as well as the core of management philosophy. The purpose of this chapter is to explore some of the management issues in preparation for the technical aspects of the subject matter which follow.

Motivation for Distributed Systems

In most organizations large enough to consider a distributed system, the evolutionary growth of computing facilities has had a tendency to disguise some important issues. In many cases, the computer was and still is used as a showpiece, in addition to providing computational services. Special computer buildings, drapery-lined viewing areas, and guided tours are commonplace. A powerful and sophisticated computer system served as evidence of a forward-looking management, where "computer success" is measured by the size of a DP budget or the number of central processing units. While, distributed systems are not a panacea for all of the world's DP problems, they do provide a means of placing the entire subject of data processing in proper perspective—in an efficient, effective, and economical manner. Some organizational structures and methods of doing business simply do not lend themselves to a distributed environment, regardless of the economic benefits.

Organizations that do opt for distributed systems, however, should do so with full realization that an effective information system is not based on raw computing power but on principles of organization. Informational resources do not depend solely on computing devices but on a conscious, deliberate, and planned set of relationships between persons, between persons and the computer resources, and between computers.

Perhaps the greatest needs of an organization are to identify its informational needs and to relate them to the organizational structure and operational procedures. Nothing is simpler to find than the informational resources at one level only. Effective management, however, requires information at several organizational levels. It follows then that one of the most difficult and recurring of management's problems is the conversion of the detailed and sometimes technical information needed in the day-to-day processes of administration into the highly digested summary information needed for policy-making decisions.

It is necessary to point out, on the other hand, that a management philosophy of distributed systems cannot in any way be based on the assumption that operational and directorial needs are in conflict. The difference is and should always be one of degree within the range of organizational objectives.

Personnel and Leadership

Modern organizations have come to recognize that managerial success is based on leadership, policy, and decision. If leadership is good, policy is sound and comprehensive, and decision is timely and appropriate, then management is regarded as effective. However, no organization can rely on supreme efforts and extraordinary talents to sustain day-to-day operations. Therefore, an organization must depend on normal individuals who have been trained and tested in that organization's primary or fundamental activities.

Thus, an organization must be organized to bring out the talents and capacities within its human resources. One of the major benefits of distributed systems is that it permits and implicitly encourages the development of key personnel with required data processing capabilities. The use of a distributed system within an organizational structure also permits individual talents to be developed as specialists and as generalists and allows managerial abilities to be tested at the local level without impacting the total organization.

From a personal point of view, working in a distributed environment with an emphasis on individual achievement provides training in two qualities: imagination and understanding. Both qualities are essential for promotion to upper levels of the organization. Through decentralization associated with distributed systems, an organization is thereby more able to produce effective data processing management than in a data processing environment that is strictly centralized.

Decentralized Organization

Based on the fairly well established assumption that the effect of data processing technology is to shift power to the department or the manager that has the computer, local management is able to behave in accordance with the basic principles of a decentralized management and organizational structure. When necessary, an executive can rely on data processing support to function as an independent businessman or to control an organizational profit center. In a centralized organizational structure, there is a tendency for the data processing department to move upward in the organization and assume a neutral stance with regard to the organization. Another way of putting the situation is that in a neutral data processing department, there may be a tendency toward "aloofness" to the needs of local management. Unfortunately, the aloofness always seems to surface during periods when the needs for data processing support are the greatest.

Clearly, systems analysis and problem definition are decentralized activities. However, the reason for decentralization of organizational structures in the first place is the lack of time for making detailed decisions, and this reason also applies to the operational aspects of data processing. The great benefit of computers to management is the reduction of slack in organizational activities, and distributed systems should reduce the slack even more.

Some of the less obvious benefits of a decentralized organization, especially with distributed systems, is the elimination of conflicts over priorities and the absence of edit management over the deployment of computer resources. In addition to speeding up the necessary computer processing, a distributed environment aims at eliminating arbitrary management whims and places data processing facilities under the objective control of cost effectiveness.

It is important to recognize that computing can only be dispersed when there is a genuine area of organizational activity to which it can be associated. There must be localized management control that can demonstrate increased effectiveness through the distributed system.

Dispersing computing facilities throughout an organization does not mean that the centralized data processing facility is weakened. On the contrary, it is a technique for strengthening the centralized data processing facility by enabling it to concentrate on its own organizational tasks and to provide overall guidance to the dispersed facilities.

In summary, a decentralized set of computer resources liberates the energies, initiative, and creativity of data processing personnel and lubricates the flow of information within an organization.

Knowledge Orientation

As computers and data processing became assimilated into organized society, there has been a steady increase in "knowledge workers," primarily concerned with information technology. There always have been the engineers, scientists, analysts, accountants, planners, and schedulers in organizations. The use of the computer has moved many more people into this category to the extent that many of them interface only with other knowledge workers and are lacking a sense of organizational purpose. The situation is not unlike monotonous blue collar activity without organizational fulfillment. The reader is reminded here of the famous "Hawthorne study" in Western Electric's Hawthorne, Illinois plant. In this study, working conditions were purposefully worsened while productivity and job satisfaction rose steadily. In short, the conclusion drawn from the work was that recognition and the importance of an individual's work to society was more significant than the work itself.

A distributed environment provides a unique opportunity to disperse the knowledge worker and provide an opportunity of interfacing with other types of activity. The notion of loyalty and accomplishment also applies to the knowledge worker in either a centralized or decentralized environment.

Policy

Policy is generally regarded as a set of principles and rules of conduct which limit and direct organizational actions and individual behavior. In short, it must be possible for the individual employee, manager, or executive to determine whether his actions are in accordance with the interests of the organization without an appeal to higher authority in each and every case.

In many cases and especially in those organizations that have a decentralized orientation, the subject of policy immediately raises questions concerning the proper balance between adherence to the principles of policy and adaptability to changing conditions. In a centralized data processing environment, policy matters that concern data processing can and frequently do have unsatisfactory consequences for local management. The lack of adaptability and the absence of timely and necessary information create dependencies on the computer that stifle initiative and creativity. In short, it is "the tail wagging the dog."

The guiding principle of policy, especially with regard to service facilities, is that it should not hinder or prevent an executive from achieving objectives for which that executive is accountable. It is poor management to decentralize without adequate operational information. As organizations expand, there is a tendency toward decentralization, so that in most cases dispersed computers provide the optimum arrangement for data processing support.

Service Staffs and the Internal Consultant

In a distributed environment, the staff of the central data processing facility has a twofold purpose. First, they provide centralized data processing support and establish data processing policy for the dispersed computing centers within the limitations inherent in local management and control. Second, and perhaps most importantly, they are the servant of the dispersed computing centers helping them to be more efficient and successful in their autonomy.

The central data processing staff thinks ahead for the total organization on data processing matters and is able to extend the planning horizon beyond what could be achieved by each and every one of the dispersed centers. Efficiency is achieved through specialization and is dispersed through internal consultants.

In a distributed environment, the internal consultant supplies local management on the average with a higher level of technical support than could have been justified locally.

A not-so-obvious benefit of the internal consultant is that the position provides a career path for the highly qualified computer specialist who declines a managerial career. Clearly, one of the major personnel problems in the computer industry relates to the rapid advances in computer technology and the large number of technical people that are seemingly content to ride the waves of evolution.

Small Is Beautiful

The phrase "Small Is Beautiful" is the title of a fairly recent contribution to the economics literature by British economist E.F. Schumacher.* The concept has great significance when related to distributed systems.

One of the key points established by Schumacher is that organizational effectiveness is a blend of order and freedom, wherein order is achieved through centralization and freedom through decentralization. One of the dangers in large-scale organization, emphasized by Schumacher, is that there is a bias and tendency toward order at the expense of freedom.

Although Schumacher recognizes that clarity and orderliness are required in any organization, there is a need for freedom to do things in a way

*The relationship of the referenced book to distributed systems was first brought to the author's attention by George Glaser in an information talk given at the annual SIGBDP "seven o'clock" meeting at the 1978 National Computer Conference.

neither anticipated nor done before. Schumacher reflects some of the issues covered previously in this chapter when he states that ". . . nobody likes to take orders from a superior who takes orders from a superior who takes orders . . . even if the rules devised by bureaucracy are outstandingly humane, nobody likes to be ruled by rules, that is to say, by people whose answer to every complaint is: 'I did not make the rules: I am merely applying them.' "[1]

In answer to the question, "What is it that we really require from the scientists and technologists?" Schumacher states that we need methods and equipment which are: (1) inexpensive enough to make them individually accessible, (2) designed for "small scale" applications, and (3) compatible with man's need for creativity.[2] Schumacher quotes Gandhi to the effect that there is a place for machines that help individuals, but that there should be no place for machines that concentrate power in a few hands and relegate the role of the masses to machine minders.

It is interesting that Schumacher essentially predicts the mini-micro computer explosion by stating the following opinion:

> If methods and machines are to be cheap enough to be generally accessible, this means that their cost must stand in some definable relationship to the level of incomes in the society in which they are to be used. I have myself come to the conclusion that the upper limit for the average amount of capital investment

[1]Schumacher, E.F., *Small Is Beautiful: Economics as if People Mattered,* (New York: Harper and Row Publishers, 1973), p. 242.

[2]Ibid, p. 34.

per workplace is probably given by the annual earnings of an able and ambitious industrial worker.[3]

In a natural and normal response to opposing forces, organizations evolve in an alternating manner through stages of centralization and decentralization. It is possible that we need both rather than either one, and distributed systems provide a means of achieving that objective.

Summary

Although the notion of a distributed system is a technological innovation, its implementation is clearly an organizational issue. One of the prime motivating forces behind distributed systems is that organizational information must exist at different levels in order to achieve effective management. Management's biggest problem in this regard is the identification of informational needs and relating them to organizational structure.

There are side benefits to the use of a distributed system. The inherent decentralization of computer facilities in a distributed system permits individual talents and capacities to be developed more fully and presents the opportunity for a higher number of leaders to be trained. Dispersed computing facilities tend to complement the efforts of local management and help in satisfying local requirements for accountability and control. A distributed system also eliminates some of the internal conflict over priorities, which are inevitable in a centralized environment, and allows policies to be established in a more equitable manner.

[3]Ibid, p. 35.

It is important to recognize that a distributed system does not necessarily imply a weakened central facility. Through the use of distributed systems, the central facility can better satisfy the needs of upper management, while supplying local service through internal consultants.

Lastly, it appears as though the notion of the decentralization of organizational structure and the dispersion of computing facilities is a partial response to an underlying social and economic need.

part two

Data Communications Concepts

4

Introduction to Data Communications

Modern society is characterized by an insatiable appetite for communications. While biological communication through nerve impulses and hormones is basic to everyday existence, communications is more commonly regarded as an external process. Some of the more common forms of human and animal communication include behavior, the written and spoken word, auditory and visual methods including the arts, and electronic methods ranging from the telegraph wire and AM radio to modern laser and optical systems. The above categories include the following:

1. Books, newspapers, periodicals
2. Radio, television, cable television
3. Verbal communication possibly including the first two categories
4. Auditory and visual recordings
5. Telegraph and telephone systems
6. Postal system
7. Computer communications

In fact, even the electrical power and transportation industries can properly be regarded as forms of communication.

Communication Systems

Much of modern communication theory is derived from the work of Claude E. Shannon, who is credited with the development of the symbolic block diagram of a communication system given in Figure 4.1. The key components in the diagram are the following:

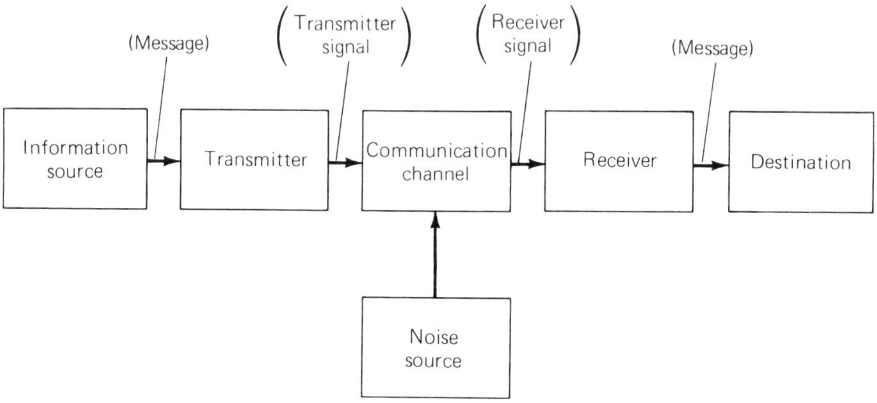

Figure 4.1: Shannon's model of the communication process

Information sources
Transmitter
Communications channel
Noise source
Receiver
Destination

This model appears to apply to all forms of communication. For example, a person (or computer) with a message to relay constitutes the starting point for a telephone system. The message is encoded and transmitted by local telephone equipment over standard telephone lines. A common noise source is the static frequently encountered during conversation. Local telephone equipment on the receiving end makes the message available to the listener (or receiving equipment).

A communication system is normally measured by the amount of information it can convey in a given period of time.

Information Flow

Through the processes of communication, information flows between transmitters and receivers. Five general patterns of information that flow in a communication system have been identified:

1. Terminal and terminal—bidirectional and simultaneous
2. Terminal and center—bidirectional with delay
3. Terminal to terminal—unidirectional with delay

4. Center to terminals—unidirectional
5. Terminals to center—unidirectional[1]

The five patterns are depicted in Figure 4.2.

In the pattern identified as *terminal and terminal—bidirectional and simultaneous,* a significant amount of delay is not permitted between terminal points in order to sustain conversation so that a bidirectional line is required, as in the telephone system. Therefore, when a connection is made between the two terminal points, a path is established between the points by a switching center as though a single connecting wire existed. (A common name for this type of communication is *line switching.*)

The pattern identified as *terminal and center—bidirectional with delay* is representative of communications systems wherein the messages are data and a few seconds delay is expected and tolerated. An on-line inquiry system, such as with airline reservations, would be modeled in this way. The delay, in this case, is necessary because of the computer processing involved. This pattern applies to almost any inquiry system regardless if a computer is involved or not.

The pattern identified as *terminal to terminal—unidirectional with delay* represents the general class of message systems, such as the manual telegraph system or a computerized store-and-forward system. This pattern is characterized by the fact that information flows between a terminal and a switching center in two directions successively —from one terminal into the center and outward from the center to a

[1]Inose, H., "Communication Networks," *Scientific American* 227: 3 (September 1972): 126.

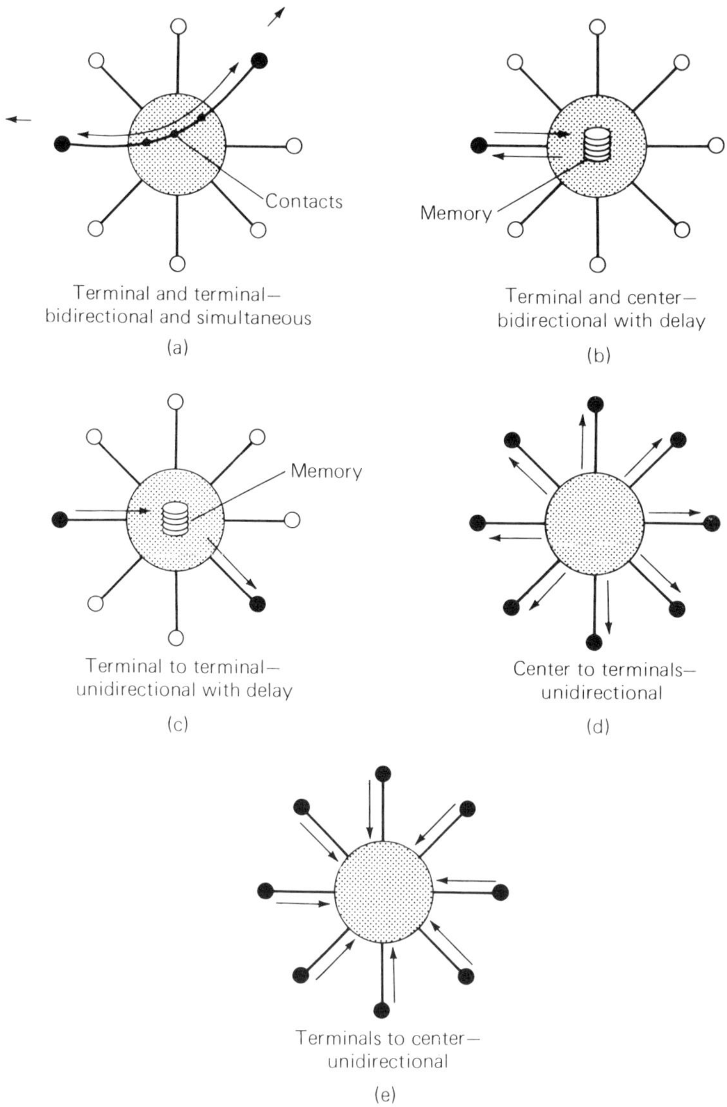

Figure 4.2: Patterns of information flow in a communication system (From "Communications Network" by H. Inose. Copyright © 1972 by Scientific American, Inc. All rights reserved.)

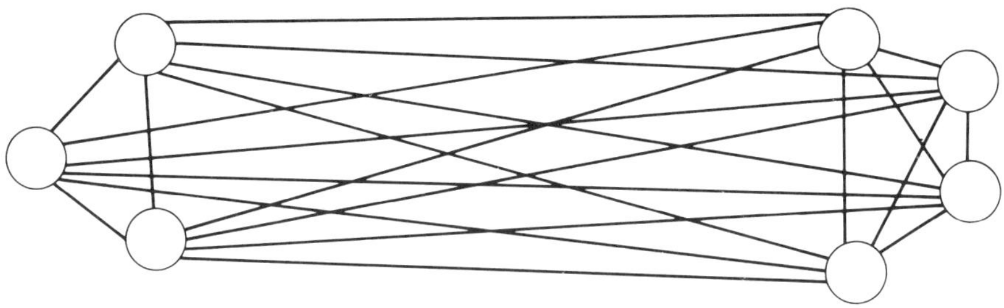

Figure 4.3: A direct connection between 7 units requires 21 wires

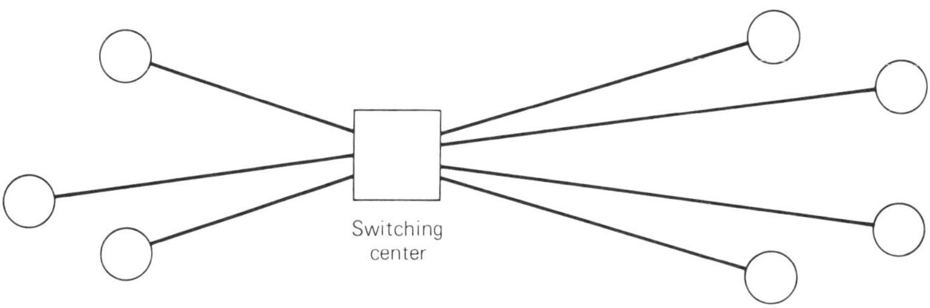

Figure 4.4: The use of a switching center reduces the number of lines to the number of units

second terminal. The delay at the switching center may range from several hours in a telegraph system to a few seconds in a computerized system. (The time necessary for the switching center to respond is usually referred to as *response time.*)

The pattern identified as *center to terminals—unidirectional* is characteristic of information dissemination systems such as radio, television, and newspaper. All mass communication takes this form as does one telecommunications system, the ALOHA system at the University of Hawaii.

The final pattern, identified as *terminals to center—unidirectional,* is representative of data collection, monitoring and reporting systems.

It is important to recognize that the flow of information in data communication systems is a combination of the basic patterns. For example, a modern computer facility may serve the following roles in addition to performing data processing tasks:

1. Remote query system (pattern 2)
2. Electronic mail system (pattern 3)
3. Data collection (pattern 5)
4. Information dissemination system (pattern 4)

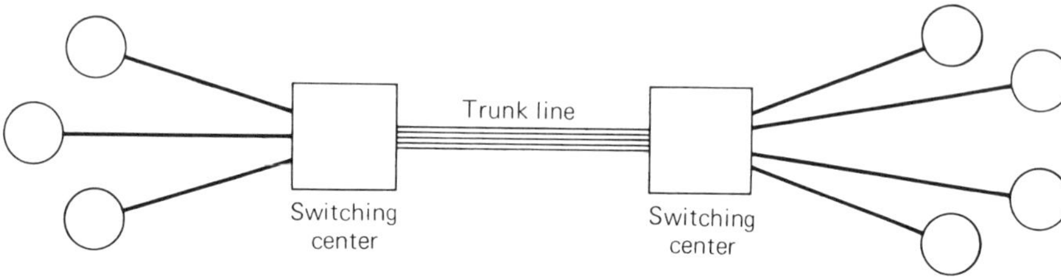

Figure 4.5: A trunk line between switching centers is used when the units are a distance apart

The consideration of information flow serves as an appropriate means of modeling data communications and distributed systems.

Switching Concepts

Regardless of the context in which it is employed and the technology used to implement it, the notion of a communications switching system is important from the standpoint of developing a data communications system. The material given here is clearly derived from the telephone system.

Consider a set of 7 units with a direct connection between them as demonstrated in Figure 4.3. (The units in this case could be telephones, computers, etc.) The method of connection would require 21 lines.* The use of a switching center, as depicted in Figure 4.4, would reduce the number of lines to 7, and if the units are a distance apart, a trunk line is used between switching centers to reduce the length of individual lines (Figure 4.5).

The preceding concepts are used in a telephone or broadcasting system, composed of a hierarchy of terminal units, end offices, toll centers, district centers, and regional centers. The local office (or end office) is used for switching at the local level. Toll, district, and regional centers serve as nodes in a distributed system. The links between the nodes are known as trunks, and as one proceeds upward in the hierarchy, the trunks have a higher data rate and a greater capacity. A distributed system of this type is depicted in Figure 4.6. When the model represents a telephone system, the pattern of information flow is "terminal and terminal—bidirectional

*$n!/k!\,(n\text{-}k)!$, where $n = 7$ and $k = 2$. (This is equivalent to $n(n\text{-}1)/2$.)

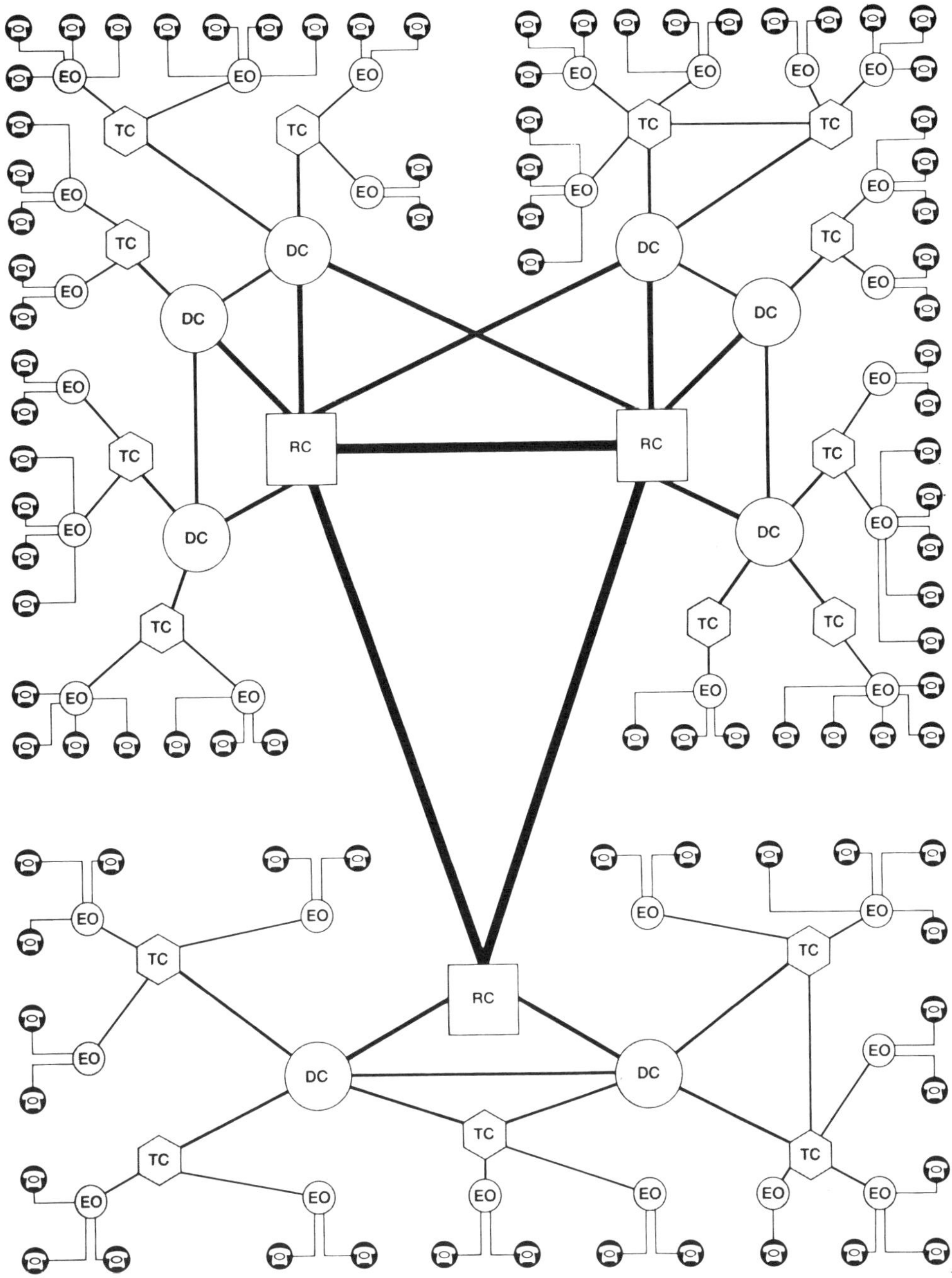

Figure 4.6: The telephone system as a distributed system (From "Communications Networks" by H. Inose. Copyright © 1972 by Scientific American, Inc. All rights reserved.)

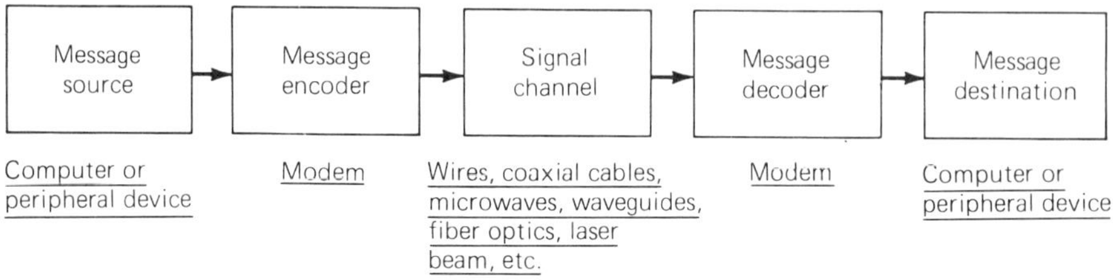

Figure 4.7: Model of a computer communications system

and simultaneous," and the terminal units are telephone receivers. When the model represents a broadcasting system, the pattern of information flow is "center to terminals—unidirectional," the nodes in the system are broadcasting stations, the links are radio waves, and the terminal units are radios or television sets.

Overview of Telecommunications

The idea of computer data communications refers to the use of ordinary telecommunications facilities, such as the telephone system, for the transmission of data between different locations. In reality, it is not significant whether the locations are in the same general vicinity or are many thousands of miles apart. Data communications facilities have been used with military/defense systems for many years in applications such as message switching, control, surveillance, and intelligence. In the computer field, data communications facilities have been used with commonplace systems as time sharing, airline reservation, and financial information.

A data communication system takes the form of Shannon's communication model given in the beginning of this chapter. Eliminating the noise source, a data communications system has five components as listed below and depicted in Figure 4.7:

1. Message source
2. Message encoder
3. Signal channel

Figure 4.8:
Classes of communications lines

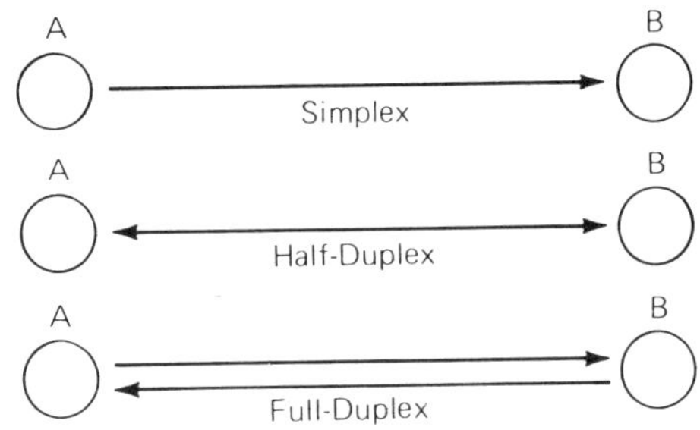

4. Message decoder
5. Message destination

The *message source* is digital computer data originating from a computer or peripheral device. A *message encoder* converts digital signals to a form suitable for telecommunications. A *signal channel* is the medium used to convey the signals and, as in telephone systems, can take any of or a combination of the following forms: wires, coaxial cables, microwaves, wave guides, or by optical means, such as fiber optics or laser beams. A *message decoder* converts telecommunications signals to digital signals, and the *message destination* is again a computer system or peripheral device.

Data Transmission

Data communications lines are classed by the direction of data transmission and relevant terminology exists. Three classes are depicted in Figure 4.8: simplex, half-duplex, and duplex. *Simplex lines* permit transmission in one direction only. *Half-duplex lines* permit transmission in either direction, but not simultaneously. *Duplex lines* permit transmission in both directions at the same time.

Computer data is represented as a train of pulses (or bits as they are usually called), wherein groups of successive pulses represent characters using an established coding system such as Baudot, USASCII, or EBC-

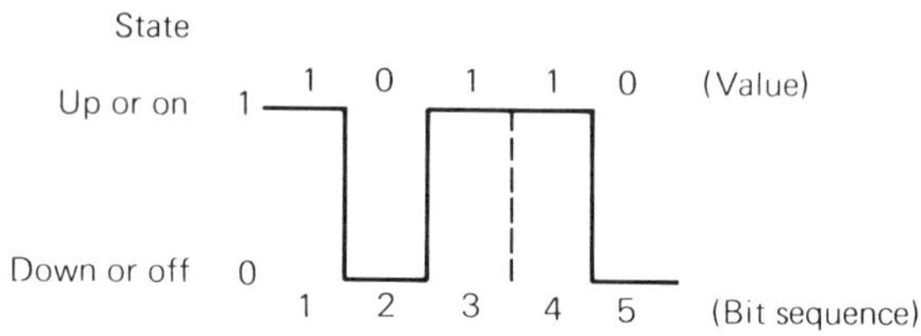

Figure 4.9: Representation of data as a bit train

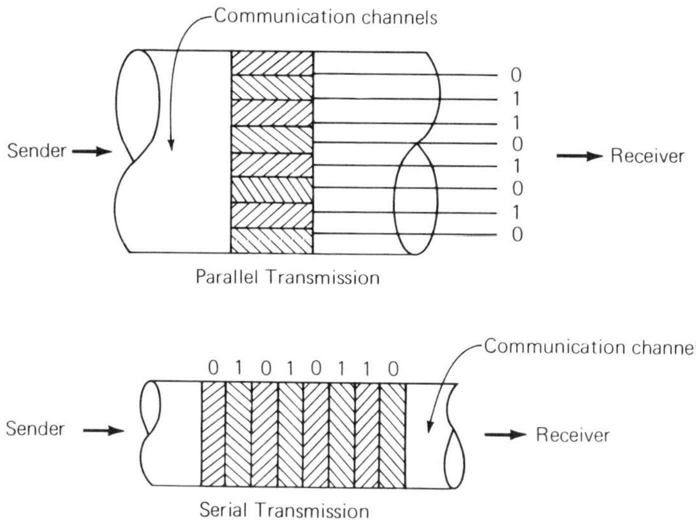

Figure 4.10: Parallel and serial transmission of an eight-bit USASCII code representing the letter V

DIC.* Figure 4.9 depicts the notion of a train of pulses, and Figure 4.10 suggests two modes of transmission: parallel and serial. With *parallel transmission,* several communication channels are used to transmit one character. With an eight-bit code, for example, eight communication channels, which may be implemented as 8 lines or 8 different frequencies on the same line, are used to send one character. The primary advantage of parallel transmission is that an entire character is transmitted in one bit time. The main disadvantage of parallel transmission is that the receiving device is relatively expensive and line costs are high.

With *serial transmission,* data is transmitted over a transmission line

*ASCII stands for United States of America Standard Code for Information Interchange, and EBCDIC stands for Extended Binary Coded Decimal Interchange Code.

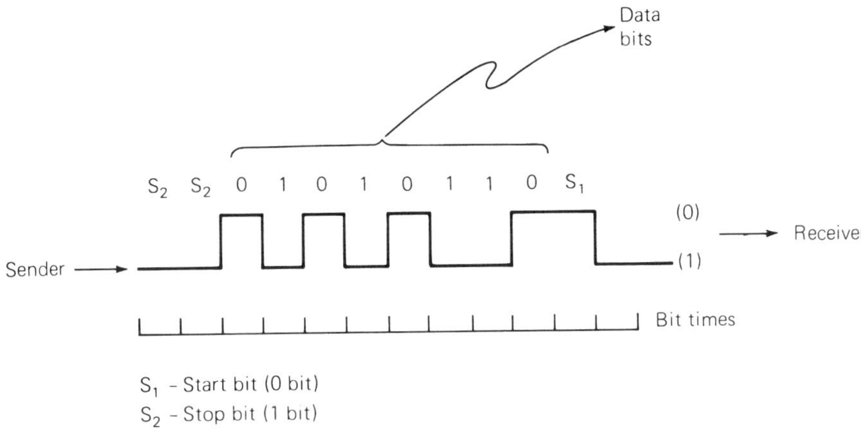

Figure 4.11: Asynchronous transmission of an eight-bit USASCII code representing the letter V

on a bit-by-bit basis. Thus, the bits in a character code are sent serially rather than simultaneously over a communications line. The serial method is the most common method of data transmission. Three serial transmission modes are used: asynchronous, synchronous, and isochronous. Asynchronous and synchronous modes are covered here. Isochronous is mentioned briefly.

In the *asynchronous mode,* each character is transmitted as a self-contained unit with start and stop bits to denote the beginning and end, respectively, of a character. The *start code* is a zero bit with a one bit-unit time duration; it signals the receiving unit to start sampling. The *stop code* is a one bit with a time duration of 1-, 1.42-, or 2- bit times;* it signals that the character is complete and resets the signal for the next character. The asynchronous mode is depicted in Figure 4.11. When a character is not being transmitted, the communications line is kept in the 1-state. Asynchronous transmission is characterized by the fact that the transmitter and receiver only involve relatively unsophisticated techniques, but requires timing for transmitter and receiver. Also, ten to eleven bits are required to transmit an eight-bit code.

In the *synchronous mode,* blocks of characters are transmitted at high speeds without start and stop codes. The transmitting and receiving devices are operated concurrently and synchronization characters are sent on a periodic basis. The sending device may transmit a long stream of data bits —one at a time. The receiving device counts the bits to establish a character and passes it to the destination. The code structure must be known by

*The stop code time duration varies depending upon the code structure and line speed.

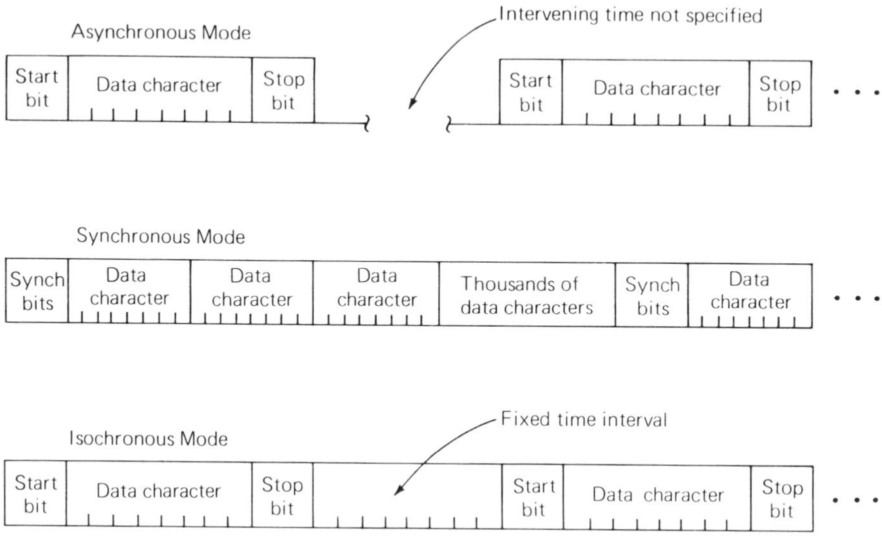

Figure 4.12: Conceptual view of the serial mode of transmission (not drawn to scale)

sending and receiving parties. Figure 4.12 gives a comparison of asynchronous, synchronous, and isochronous modes.

The *isochronous mode* of serial data transmission combines the advantages of asynchronous and synchronous transmission. Start and stop bits are used as in asynchronous transmission, but also, the transmitter and receiver are synchronized as in synchronous transmission. The primary advantage of isochronous transmission is that it permits higher data rates than asynchronous transmission.

Signal Representation

Most communication lines used for data transmission are designed to carry analog signals, however, computer data is digital data so that a technique must be used for representing a digital signal on an analog signal.

The basis of an analog signal is a continuous oscillating voltage, known as a *carrier signal,* that carries no information. The amplitude and frequency of a carrier signal is fixed for a given communications line, and information is transmitted over that line by altering one of the characteristics of its carrier signal. The process of modifying a characteristic of a carrier signal to transmit information is called *modulation,* and three common methods of modulation are amplitude modulation, frequency modulation, and phase modulation.

The process of modulating a signal to carry information is conceptual-

Figure 4.13: Modulation

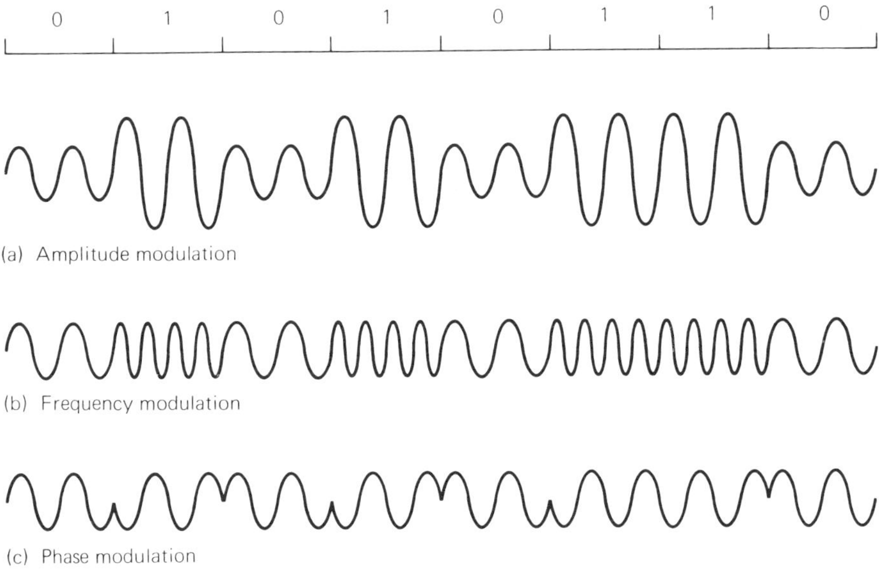

Figure 4.14: Amplitude, frequency and phase modulation

ized in Figure 4.13. Modulation and demodulation are performed with a device called a *modem,* which is an acronym for *mo*dulator and *dem*odulator.

In *amplitude modulation,* the amplitude of the carrier signal is varied to represent information, as shown in Figure 4.14a. In *frequency modulation,* the frequency of the carrier signal is varied to represent information, as shown in Figure 4.14b. In *phase modulation,* the phase of the carrier signal is shifted to represent information, as shown in part (c).

Summary

Communication can take many forms and utilize a variety of media. In fact, much of our everyday behavior involves communications—in one form or another. Most if not all communication adheres to Shannon's general model of a communication system that includes the following components: information source, transmitter, communications channel, noise source, receiver, and destination.

Much like the general model of a communication system, information flow in communication systems also follows general patterns. Five patterns are identified: terminal and terminal, terminal and center, terminal to terminal, center to terminals, and terminals to center. The five patterns apply not only to societal communications but to data communication systems as well.

Communications are implemented through switching systems that permit connections to be made between a sender and receiver and involve ordinary telecommunications facilities in computer data communications systems. Data communications lines are classed as simplex, half-duplex, and duplex; in each case, the classification is determined by the direction of data flow. Signals can be transmitted serially or in parallel. In data communications, serial transmission is normally used and three modes are identified: asynchronous, synchronous, and isochronous. Data are represented on an analog signal through the process of modulation, which can involve any of three general methods: amplitude modulation, frequency modulation, and phase modulation.

5

Computer Networks

This chapter covers the utilization of data communications technology in the development of computer networks, which are the essential parts of the various kinds of distributed systems. The use of computer networks provides the capability for effective and efficient management through the timely exchange of data between remote facilities and the sharing of computer resources. Overall, computer networks are most frequently used for data processing, information distribution, and data collection. The idea of a network is not new, with notable examples being the rail, highway, power distribution, and international telephone systems. While most networks, such as the examples given above, require the coordinated activity of several groups, organizations, or a government, a computer network is unique in the sense that it can be designed, implemented, and used by an independent organization.

Objectives of Computer Networks

A *computer network* is a collection of computers and terminal devices connected together by a communication system. The set of computers may include large-scale computers, medium-scale computers, minicomputers, and microcomputers. The set of terminal devices may include intelligent terminals, "dumb" terminals, work stations of various kinds, and miscellaneous devices such as the commonly used telephone instrument.

Many computer people feel that a computer network must include more than one computer system—otherwise, it is an ordinary on-line system. Others feel that the use of telecommunications facilities is of primary importance and the concept is a very general one, which includes time sharing, on-line systems, RJE systems,* and so forth. The key point has been made. There is no specific definition of a computer network.

One good method of characterizing a computer network is to discuss the reasons for which it is used or the facilities that it provides. In addition to increasing the reliability of computer resources and facilitating overall systems development,† computer networks satisfy the primary objective of resource sharing, which includes device sharing, file sharing, program sharing, and program segmentation.

Device sharing permits a remote device to be used as though it were connected to a local computer system. *File sharing* permits data to be exchanged among remote computer systems and accessed as though it were stored locally. *Program sharing* permits a program to be transmitted to a remote computer system and then loaded and executed by that computer system. *Program segmentation* refers to the process of dividing an executable procedure into independent tasks, having the tasks executed on different computer systems, and then coordinating the various diverse activities.

Basic Network Terminology and Topology

The geometrical arrangement of computer resources, remote devices, and communication facilities is known as *network topology.* More specifically,

*RJE is an acronym for Remote Job Entry.

†This is true because a system can be designed, implemented, tested, and installed on a piecemeal basis.

a computer network is comprised of nodes and links. A *node* is the end point of any branch in a computer network and can take the form of a computer, a terminal device, work station, a miscellaneous device as mentioned above, or an interconnecting equipment facility. A *link* is a communication path between two nodes. (The terms "circuit" and "channel" are frequently used as synonyms for link.) When a computer network is designed, its topology is determined by the following considerations: functional objectives, reliability requirements, operational costs. There is no standard network topology even though general configurations, covered in a later section, have been identified.

Two basic network types are available through data communications technology: point-to-point and multipoint. In a *point-to-point connection,* two nodes are connected through a single communications link, such that one communications channel exists for that link. The communications link may be a private line or a switched line established through a dial-up method. The nodes in a point-to-point connection may be two computers, two peripheral devices or work stations, or a computer and either a peripheral device or work station. In a *multipoint connection,** several nodes share the same communication link, but only one node can transmit at a time. Onc node is designated as the control station and it is used to poll the other nodes, designated as tributary stations. The control station is usually a computer and the tributary stations may be computers, peripheral devices, or work stations. Polling systems normally require nonswitched lines. Figure 5.1 depicts basic network topology.

*The word "multidrop" is frequently used as a synonym for multipoint.

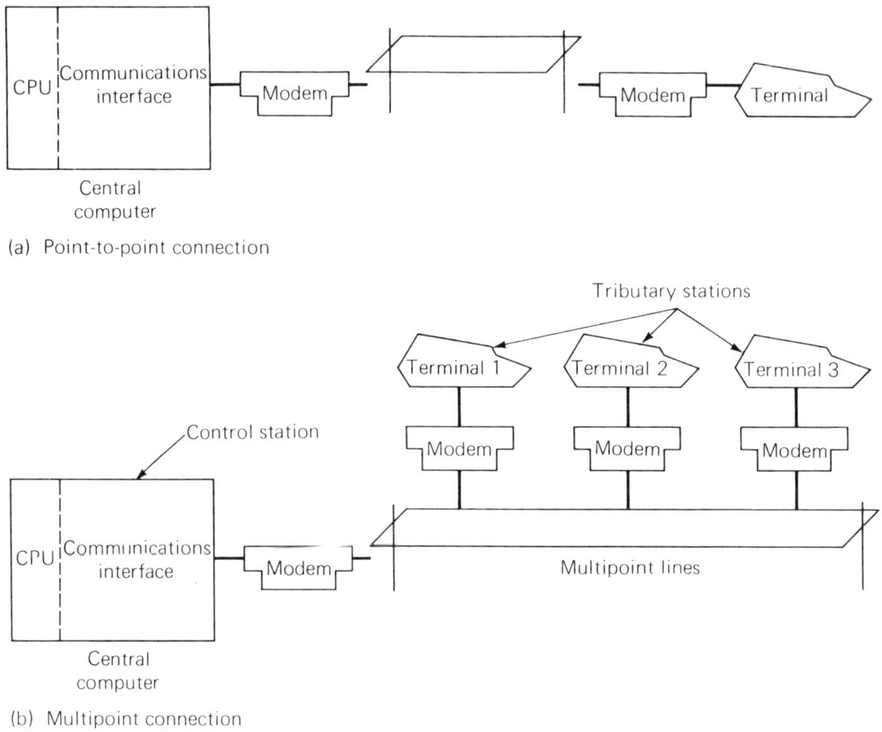

Figure 5.1: Basic network topology

In a multipoint connection, each tributary station has an address and is designed to recognize and respond to that address. Thus, the control station can send a message down the line addressed to a specific tributary station and only that station will respond. In a sense, each tributary station listens on the line for its own address.

Classification of Computer Networks for Distributed Systems

Aside from network topology, which is covered in more detail later, computer networks can be classified on the basis of the manner in which they contribute to the design of a distributed system. Three network concepts are identified as centralized, distributed, and value added.

A *centralized computer network,* which is depicted in Figure 5.2, is characterized by a centralized computer complex, a communications system, and a set of users that can interact with the computer system via local terminal devices. The term "centralized" also refers to a network topology, covered later, and the meanings are similar.

Figure 5.2: Conceptual view of a centralized computer network

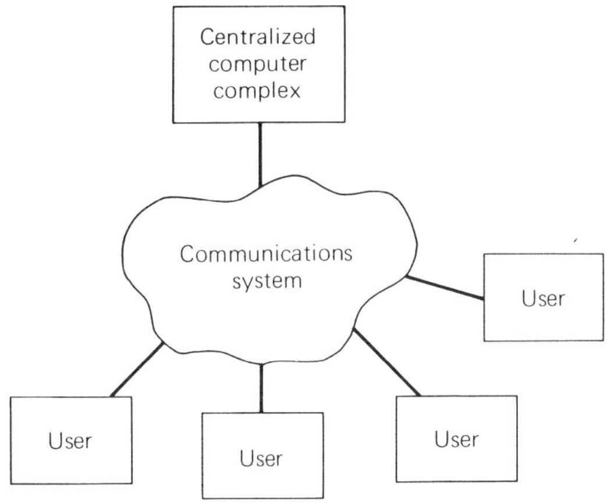

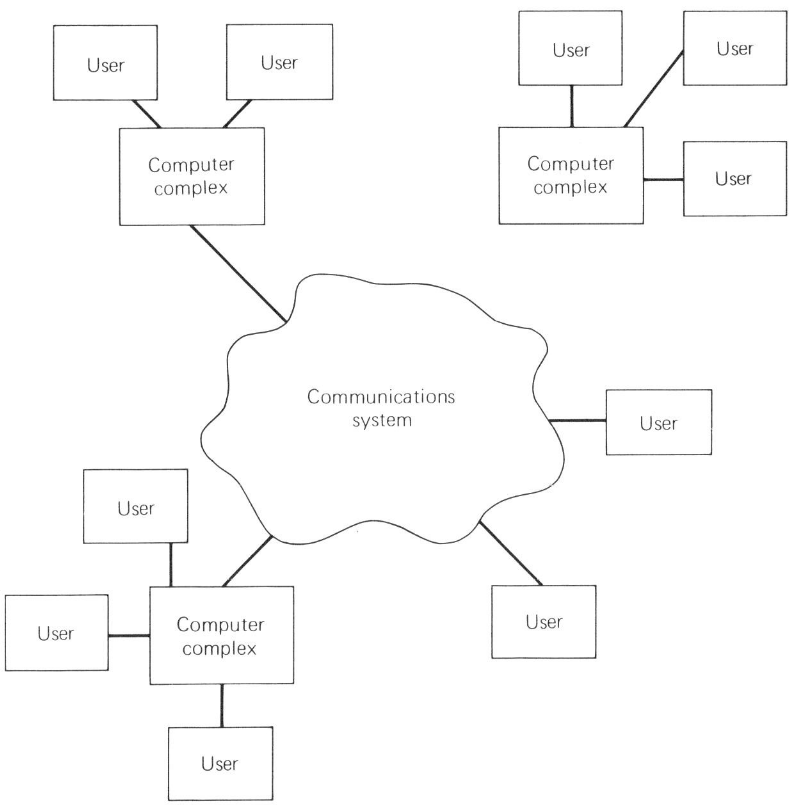

Figure 5.3: Conceptual view of a distributed computer network

A *distributed computer network,* which is depicted in Figure 5.3, is characterized by two or more computer complexes that are connected by a communications system. Users can interact with one of the computer complexes via local telecommunications facilities or can be connected to the communication system itself and interact with any of the computer complexes. When the term "computer network" is used, a distributed computer network is usually the intended meaning. To sum up, two or more distinct computer complexes connected via telecommunications facilities is referred to as a "communications based" system that satisfies the basic definition of a distributed computer network. Two or more computer complexes connected by data buses is referred to as a "bus based" system that does not satisfy the basic definition of a distributed computer network.

One means of offsetting the start-up costs of a computer network is to share a set of telecommunications facilities with other organizations. Heretofore, computer network capability has been available for economic reasons only to specialized organizations, such as airlines, banking institutions, and large corporations. A *value-added network* is a public network service that builds on existing telecommunications facilities by providing a means of connecting a user's communications equipment to the network, by routing messages between locations, and by guaranteeing message integrity. Value-added network capability is a service for which a customer is charged a dollar amount by a service company that effectively "owns the network." Customers that use a value-added network are effectively pooling resources, and small customers can utilize a computer network without having to finance the entire system. It is important to recognize with a

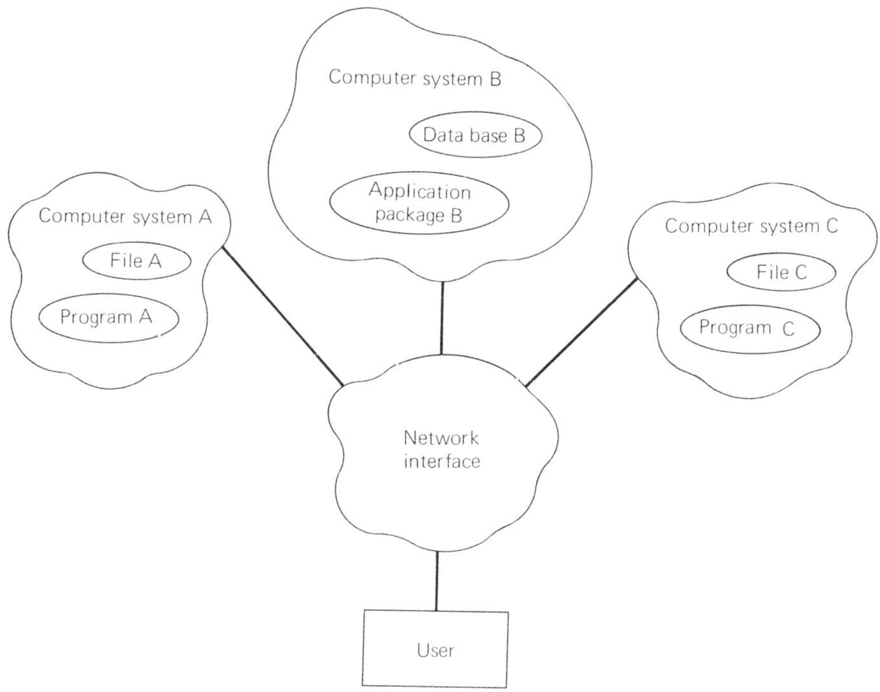

Figure 5.4: Conceptual view of a computer communications system

value-added network that all a customer need do is connect to the network and the service company supplies the telecommunications capability.

User Classification of Computer Networks

Another useful classification of a computer network is based on how an end user might view it. A user may view a computer network as a single computer system or as a set of computer systems.

Figure 5.4 depicts a *computer-communications system.* In it, the user views the computer network as a set of separate computer systems. Access to the network is through a local network interface. Nevertheless, the user explicitly chooses a specific computer system for service and interacts with that system with its local operating conventions after the connection is established.

Figure 5.5 depicts a *network computer system.* In it, the user views the computer network as one large computer system, even though the computer network is comprised of several separate computer systems. The computer system on which a program is executed or from which data is

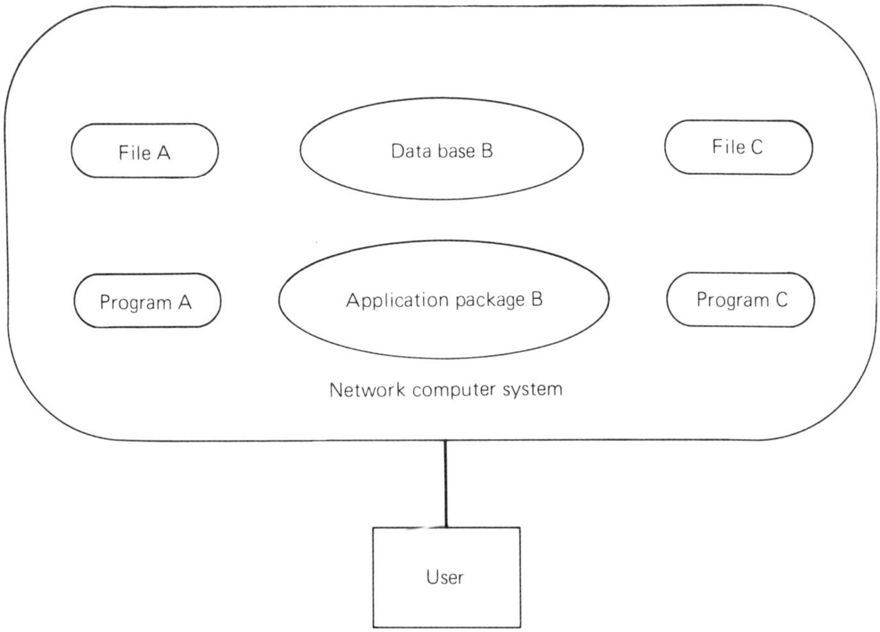

Figure 5.5: Conceptual view of a network computer system

accessed is transparent to the user, who interacts with the network computer system with a standard set of operating conventions.

Network Structures

The manner in which networks are actually connected utilizes a combination of the basic network topologies given earlier. A network structure effectively determines which elements in a computer network can communicate with each other. Figure 5.6 suggests a hypothetical network model. Six network structures are identified: centralized-star, hierarchical, distributed, fully distributed, multistar, and ring.

The *centralized network structure* (also known as the *star network*) is characterized by communication channels emanating from a centralized computer system, as suggested by Figure 5.7. The information flow in a star network is "terminal and center—bidirectional with delay" and "terminal to terminal—unidirectional with delay." A centralized network is particularly appropriate for organizations that require a centralized data base or a centralized processing facility. As examples, a star network might be used in retailing for centralized inventory control and in banking for centralized record keeping in an on-line branch office environment.

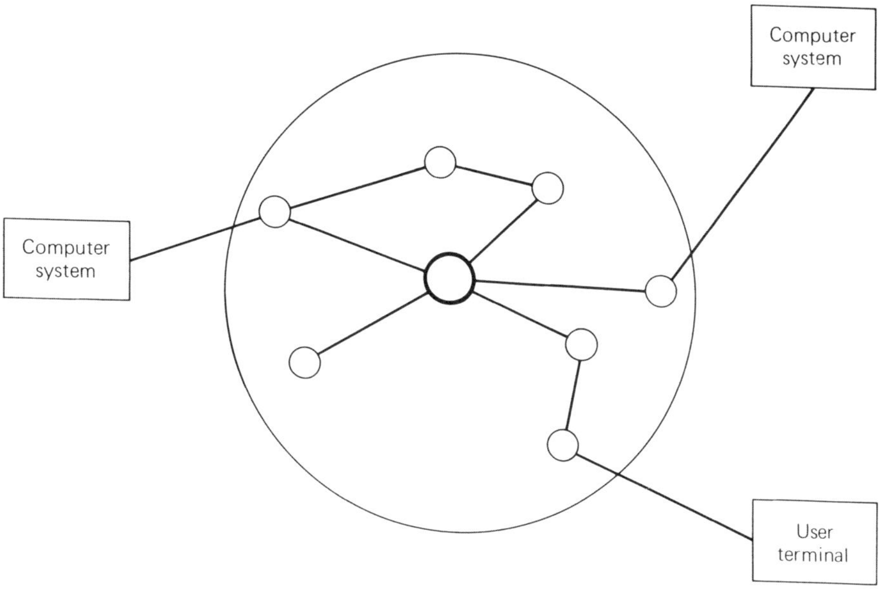

Figure 5.6: A hypothetical network model

A *hierarchical network structure* is a slight variation to the star network—in fact, their topologies are identical—in which function is associated with distance in nodes from the central node. Figure 5.8 depicts a hierarchical network structure, composed of multilevels consisting of a central computer system, front-end computers, concentrators, multiplexers, and terminals. Each of the network components is covered in a later chapter. Real-time or on-line systems, as with airline reservations systems, lend themselves to a hierarchical network structure.

A *distributed network structure* is characterized by multiple connections between nodes, which are usually taken to be computer systems rather than network elements. Figure 5.9 demonstrates a distributed network structure. The level of connectivity of a distributed network structure is the average number of connection links connected to a node. In the network of Figure 5.9, for example, the level of connectivity is 3. An important consideration in a distributed network is its tolerance to circuit failure, so that the reliability of a network is dependent upon the availability of alternate routes if a primary link is disrupted. The *cut set* of a network is the minimum number of circuits that must be disrupted (i.e., cut) to partition the network. An example of an organization that might use a distributed network structure would be a large manufacturing corporation requiring computer facilities in remote plants that communicate and coordinate on a regular basis.

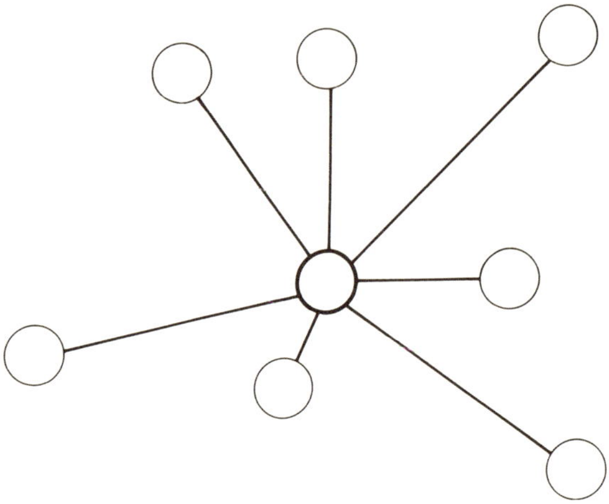

Figure 5.7: Centralized network structure (also known as a star network)

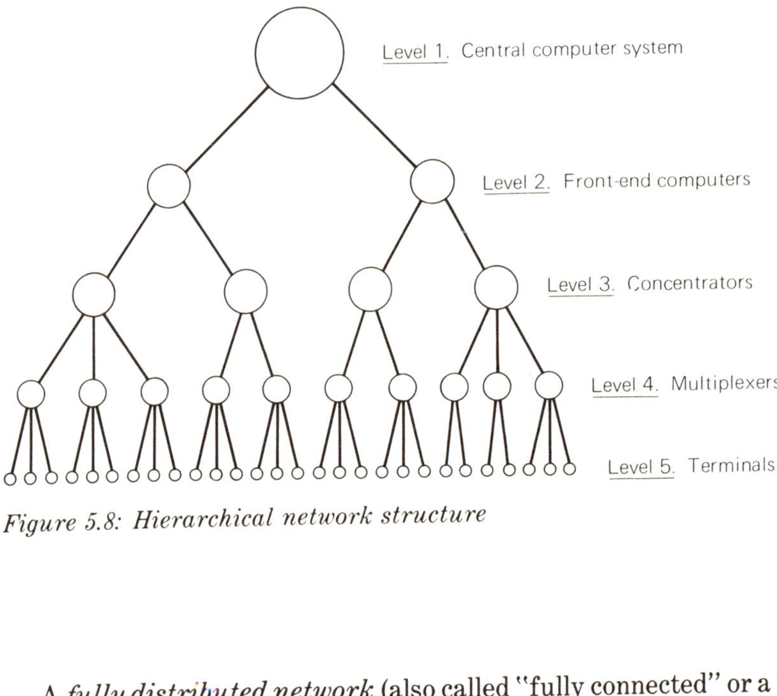

Figure 5.8: Hierarchical network structure

A *fully distributed network* (also called "fully connected" or a network with full connectivity) exists when every node can communicate directly with every other node. A fully distributed network is impractical because of the number of connectives (i.e., $n(n\text{-}1)/2$, where n is the number of nodes), except for small networks, but offers the advantage that software is not required for making routing decisions.

A *multistar network structure* is a distributed network structure in which nodes are centralized subnetworks, as shown in Figure 5.10. A net-

Figure 5.9: Distributed network structure

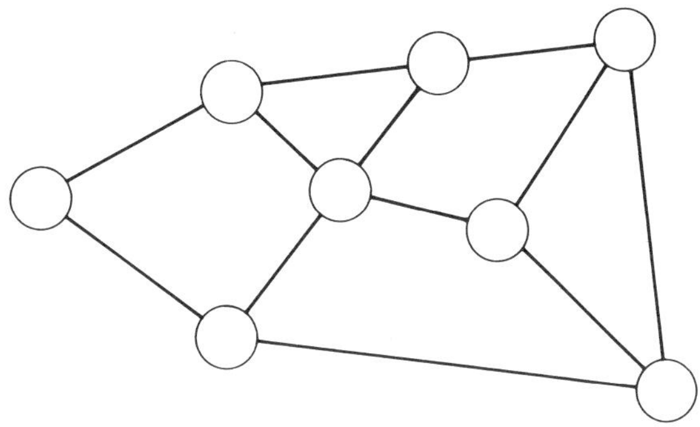

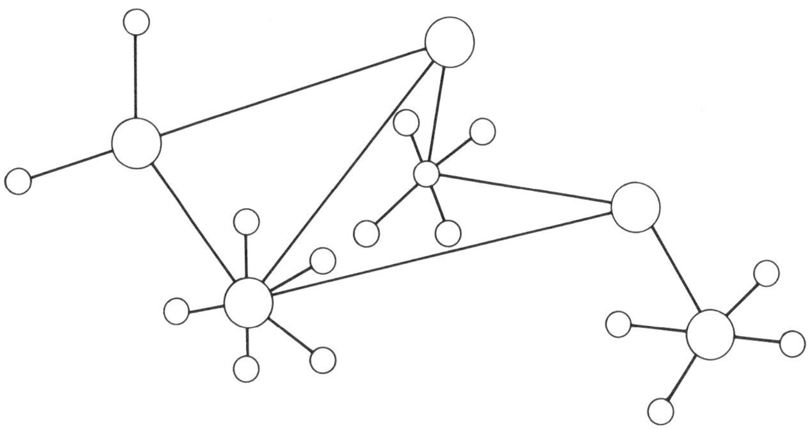

Figure 5.10: A multistar network structure

work system, such as ARPANET as introduced in the second chapter, is an example of a multistar network structure. A more specific example might be a network of time-sharing systems.

A *ring network structure* is a special case of a distributed network structure in which every node is connected to exactly two other systems (Figure 5.11). A ring network structure is frequently associated with a decentralized organizational structure in which coordination and communication between systems is needed but not on a regular basis.

Network Composition and Design

In a computer network, the component systems (or nodes, as they are frequently called) can be the same or different. This is clearly a matter of level and degree, but the resulting terminology is useful for discursive

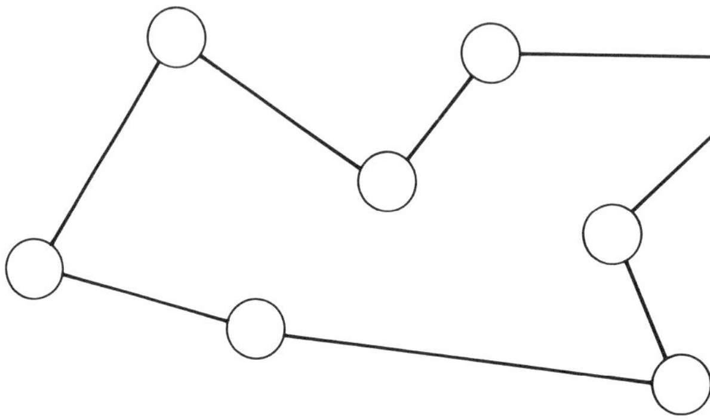

Figure 5.11: Ring network structure

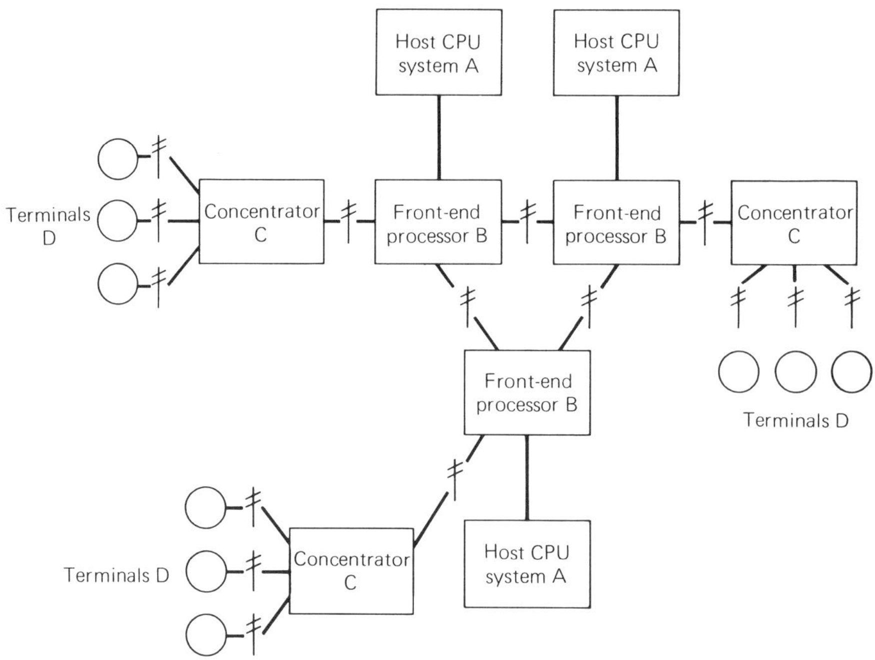

Figure 5.12: Each host CPU system is the same—hence a homogeneous system. At the individual component level, however, hardware is different and could be regarded as heterogeneous.

purposes. In a *homogeneous system,* each component computer system is "essentially" the same, in terms of model and computational and storage capability. In a *heterogeneous system,* different models of computers are employed. In Figure 5.12, for example, each host-CPU system is the same so the system could be regarded as homogeneous. On the other hand, if the analysis were made at the individual hardware component level, it would be a heterogeneous system.

Another element in network design is the manner in which the processing of work is performed by the computer systems in the network. Three classifications based on work processing are identified: utilitarian, task, and functional. In general, the method of work processing is independent of the topological arrangement of node in the network structure.

On a *utilitarian network,* a unit of work is performed in its entirety on the same kind of computer system—even though access, input, and output may have been made possible through the network communication system. Off-loading may take place for reasons of efficiency or convenience, and this is simply taken to mean that a unit of work is started on one computer system and is completed on another computer system. A utilitarian processing environment is depicted in Figure 5.13. Off-loading in this manner may require that the system be homogeneous or heterogeneous, depending upon how the unit of work is partitioned.

On a *task network,* a single unit of work is partitioned between two or more computer systems. The task that is executed on a given computer system is preassigned to that system based on its configuration and operational characteristics. A unit of work is then passed among various computer systems, based on its processing requirements. A "high performance" network may be organized in such a manner that specific computer systems have a specialization; for example, compilation, data base updating and retrieval, and on-line control may be typical "specializations." Figure 5.14 demonstrates a hypothetical task network.

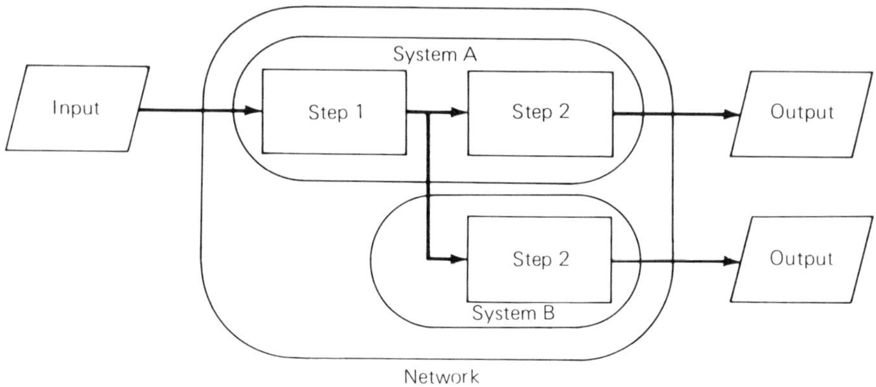

Figure 5.13: Utilitarian network

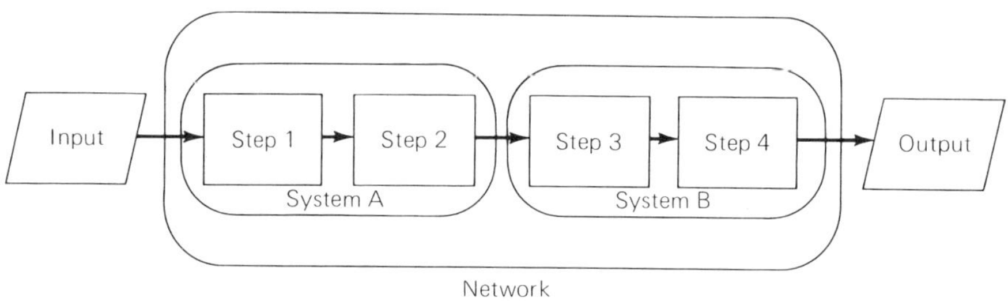

Figure 5.14: Task network

A small on-site computer in a *functional network* provides access to the processing of the network but does not perform a significant amount of processing. Figure 5.15 depicts this type of network. A point-of-sale (POS) terminal connected to a minicomputer in a retail store and a RJE/RJO computer* are common examples of functional network concepts.

Network Switching and Routing

An important concept in computer networks is the set of techniques used for routing messages from source to destination. Essentially, three techniques are used: circuit switching, message switching, and broadcasting. Several variations also exist.

The most common form of network switching uses the public telephone network and is called *circuit switching.* With circuit switching, a physical connection exists for the duration of a connection, and once that connection

*RJE/RJO is an acronym for Remote Job Entry/Remote Job Output.

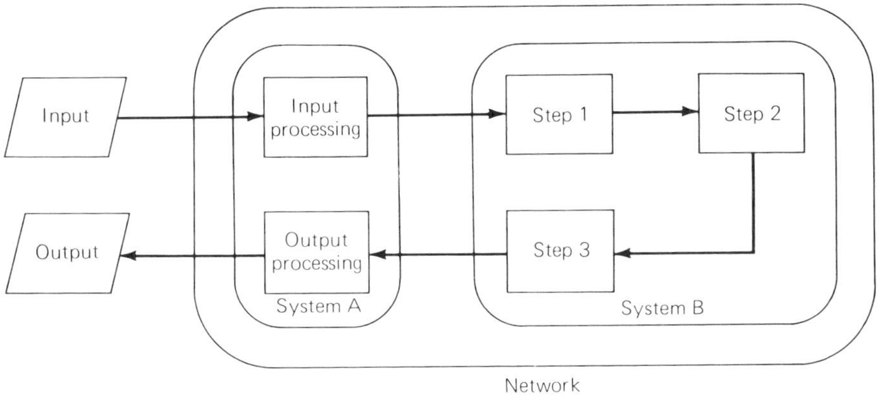

Figure 5.15: Functional network

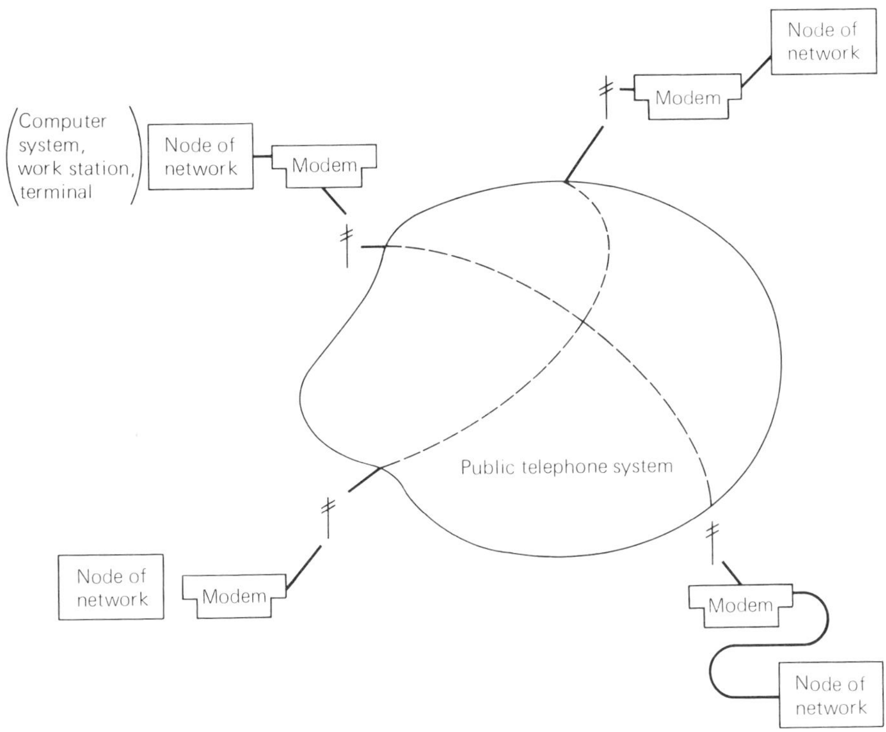

Figure 5.16: Circuit switching

is established, there is essentially no delay in transmission. A circuit switching setup is conceptualized in Figure 5.16. This type of switching ties up a physical connection for the duration of a session (called *holding time*), and all messages take the same path from source to destination.

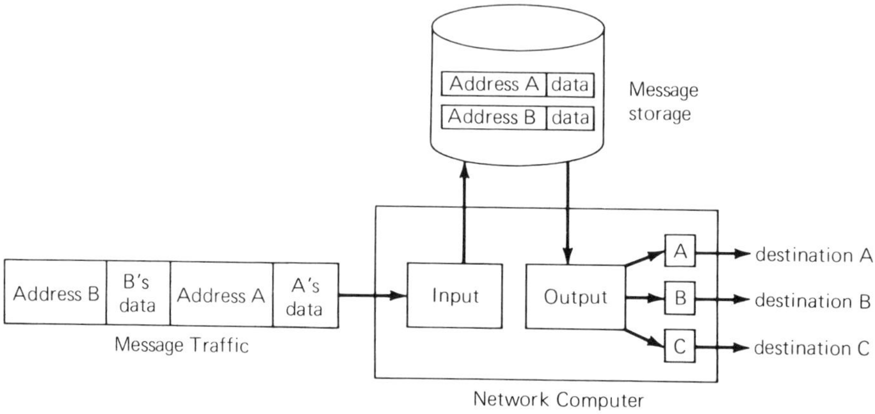

Figure 5.17: Conceptual view of message switching

With *message switching,* no circuit is established between source and destination and messages are transmitted as a unit between nodes in a network. Each message, therefore, contains an address that determines its eventual destination in the network. Based on the address, each node can determine where to forward the message. Because there may be delays because of message traffic, messages are frequently stored until a "node to node" connection can be established, and as a result, message switching systems are sometimes referred to as *store-and-forward systems.* Normally, there are many possible different paths in a network between nodes so subsequent messages may take different routes. A message switching system is conceptualized in Figure 5.17. Minicomputers are frequently used in message switching systems as "network computers" for receiving, storing, and forwarding messages.

Another technique which has limited utilization thus far is *broadcasting,* as used with the ALOHA system at the University of Hawaii. In a broadcasting system, all messages are broadcast on the same medium—which was a satellite in the ALOHA system. Each message, received by all stations, contains a unique address representing its destination. A filter at each station identifies its messages and permits their reception. With several stations broadcasting at the same time, conflicts can occur so that retransmission is required during periods of high activity. More specifically, each received message is acknowledged. Therefore, if an acknowledgment for a transmitted message is not received within a specified time interval, it is automatically rebroadcast.

One of the knotty problems in computer networks involves the handling of messages with different attributes. This situation results in cumbersome

Figure 5.18: Hypothetical packet switching system implemented as a ring network structure

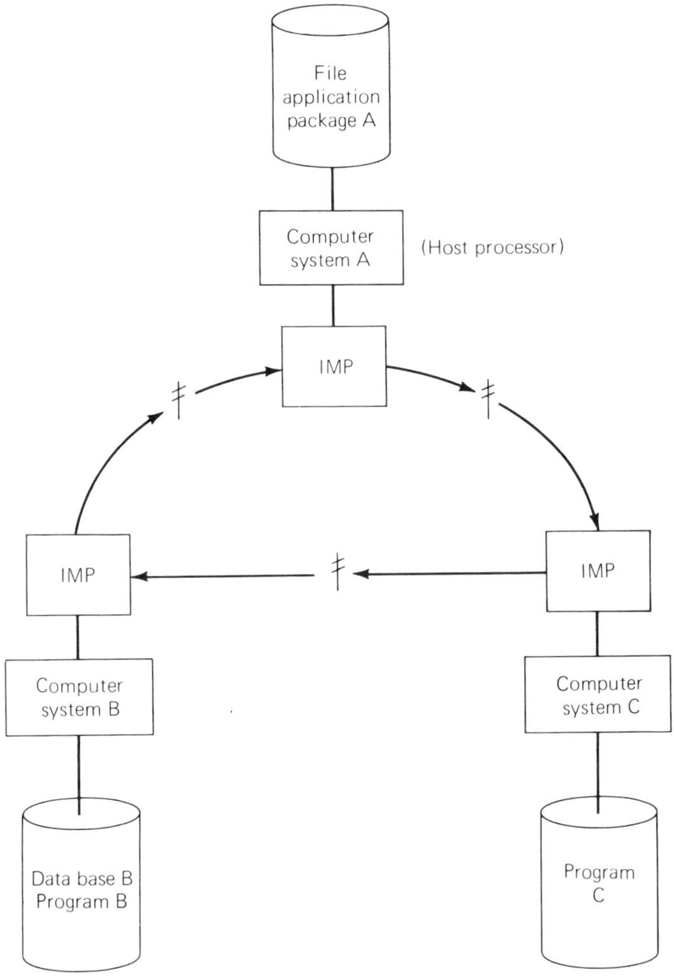

data management problems. An established technique for the switching of messages with different record lengths is to transmit them between nodes in fixed sized blocks,* termed "packets." A *packet* is a fixed block size—such as 1024 bits (i.e., 128 characters of information)—that is used as the standard unit of transfer over the message system. Placed in proper perspective, packet switching is a subset of message switching. From a data management point of view, a packet is a set of blocked records or a part

*The use of packets is roughly analogous to the use of spanned records in some data management systems.

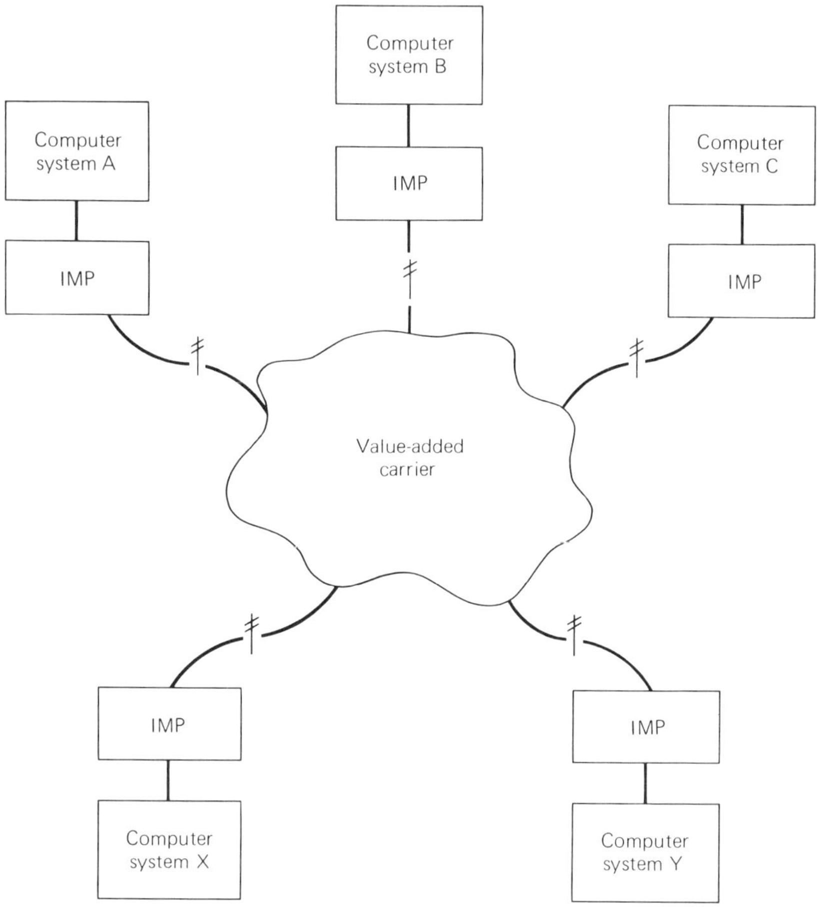

Figure 5.19: Logical circuit using a value-added carrier

of a longer record, depending upon the message sizes. Figure 5.18 depicts a hypothetical packet switching system that uses a store-and-forward minicomputer known as an *interface message processor* (IMP). The IMP coordinates with its host computer system and performs three major functions:

1. Puts packets into the network from its host
2. Takes packets from the network for its host
3. Receives and forwards packets from the network for other hosts

In a packet switching system, no provision is made for the long-term storage of packets and they are forwarded as they are received. Thus, the IMPs play a major role in packet switching system operation.

In a packet switching system, a logical circuit may be effectively established between two nonadjacent systems, as in Figure 5.19 with computer

Table 5.1: Conceptual mapping table for a virtual circuit

INPUT PORT	OUTPUT PORT
A	Y
B	Y
C	X

systems C and X, through the use of a value-added carrier. Clearly, physical circuits exist in the network and as access lines from a local IMP to the network. Between any two stations, such as C and X in this case, there appears to be a circuit established, but in reality the physical circuits are shared with other subscribers. A circuit of this type is known as a *virtual circuit,* which exists for the duration of a connection and uses a mapping table in a minicomputer, which is part of the value-added carrier network. Table 5.1 gives a conceptual mapping table for a virtual circuit.

Summary

A computer network is a collection of computers and terminal devices connected together by a communications system. Because no specific definition of the precise composition of a computer network exists, several methods of characterization are used. One characterization involves the reasons for which a network is used and includes computer resource sharing, file sharing, program sharing, and program segmentation. The geometrical arrangement of computer resources, remote devices, and communication facilities is known as network topology. A network topology is based on either a point-to-point or a multipoint connection.

Network concepts can be classed depending upon how they contribute to the design of a distributed system. Three concepts are identified: centralized, distributed, and value added. A user, on the other hand, may classify a computer network as a single computer system or as a set of computer systems and this classification determines how the computer network is accessed.

Network structures build on the basic network topology and include the centralized-star, hierarchical, distributed, fully distributed, multistar, and ring.

The manner in which work is partitioned in a computer network determines essentially how effectively the resources of the network are utilized. With a utilitarian network, a single unit of work is performed entirely on one computer system with off-loading as required. With a task network, a single unit of work is partitioned between two or more computer systems. The various computer systems in the computer network are configured to execute specific tasks, such as compilation or data base processing. With a functional network, a small on-site computer provides access to the network but does not perform a significant amount of processing.

The techniques in a computer network for routing messages from source to destination are generally classed as circuit switching, message switching, and broadcasting. Through one or more of the above techniques, many computer networks provide packet switching capability and virtual circuits.

6

Network Functions and Components

In order to provide the data communication capability introduced in chapters 4 and 5, the computer network itself is a type of processing system. As such, the computer network, as a whole, performs a set of well-defined functions. In so doing, it uses a set of network components, and adheres to a collection of rules or procedures. The components are also called network elements and include hardware items, such as central computers, front-end processors, concentrators, multiplexers, work stations, intelligent terminals, and several miscellaneous devices.

Network Functions

The process of sustaining the operation of a computer network involves considerably more identifiable functions than most users realize. Some functions are taken for granted, and others are generally not known to exist. The network functions identified here are:

Host processing
Front-end processing
Connection
Switching and flow control
Routing
Measurement
Polling
Conditioning and equalizing
Multiplexing
Concentration

The network components that perform the above functions are covered in a subsequent section.

HOST PROCESSING. This function applies to computer networks that perform services other than network control—such as a value-added network. Host processing may involve time-sharing service, an on-line information resource, data processing, data base updating and retrieval, scientific computing and problem solving, process control, or any combination thereof.

FRONT-END PROCESSING. This function, sometimes referred to as "communications processing," involves communication tasks such as line control, error checking, code conversion, polling, addressing, message assembly and disassembly, automatic answering, and maintenance of network processing in the event of host system failure. Front-end processing may also include standard data processing, special interfacing between terminal and host, and performance monitoring and evaluation.

CONNECTION. When switching computers, such as the interface message processor (IMP) covered in chapter 5, are used in a computer network, then a necessary network function is the initiation of an initial connection between processors. This function may involve automatic dialing and answering and may establish a connection for the duration of a session or for the forwarding and storage of a single message.

SWITCHING AND FLOW CONTROL. In systems where physical circuits exist for the duration of a session, then the switching and flow control function is effectively performed during connection. When message switching is required, then it is necessary that messages be stored and forwarded in the proper sequence. This process may involve polling, code conversion, message assembly and disassembly, line control, speed conversion, error control, time stamping, date stamping, and message header analysis. Facilities are normally available for storing messages for a short time (such as a few seconds) and for an extended period (such as a day or more).

ROUTING. This function is necessary when there is more than one path for a message from source to destination in a network. Tables containing physical path data are used for this function with three major objectives: minimizing transit time, equalizing the load on the physical circuits, and adapting to circuit failures. In a distributed network structure, this function may be performed at each node in the network. In a centralized network structure, this function is performed at the central computer system.

MEASUREMENT. This function involves the collection of statistics to aid in determining the effectiveness of the computer network from a performance standpoint and the proper utilization of network resources. Items measured would include queue lengths, traffic control, message size, and error occurrences.

POLLING. This function is a technique for controlling line utilization by having a central computer or control station solicit messages from tributary stations. Using a predefined discipline, the polling station sends a message to each polled station on a periodic basis inviting it to transmit a message. If the tributary station has a message to transmit, it is sent to the polling station. Otherwise, it replies that it has nothing to transmit. The result of polling is that several stations can share a common communications line.

CONDITIONING AND EQUALIZING. This function compensates for the distortion of an analog signal due to distance. Two kinds of distortion are involved: attenuation and phase shift—both proportional to frequency. Compensation for this distortion can be performed by adding complementary filters. Conditioning occurs when the filter is added to the physical plant. Equalizing occurs when the filter is added to the modem.

MULTIPLEXING. This function permits several low-speed devices to share a higher-capacity data link and thereby take advantage of the lower cost per bit associated with the higher-capacity facilities. Figure 6.1 gives an example of multiplexing. Multiplexing techniques are designed to utilize the available channel capacity and is normally available through a hardwired device. The diagram in Figure 6.1 reflects a typical use of multiplexers by time-sharing service companies. In order to obtain customers, most time-sharing service companies place multiplexers in key locations so that customers can tie into the service with a local call. The time-sharing service company effectively subsidizes the line charges by paying for the multiplex-

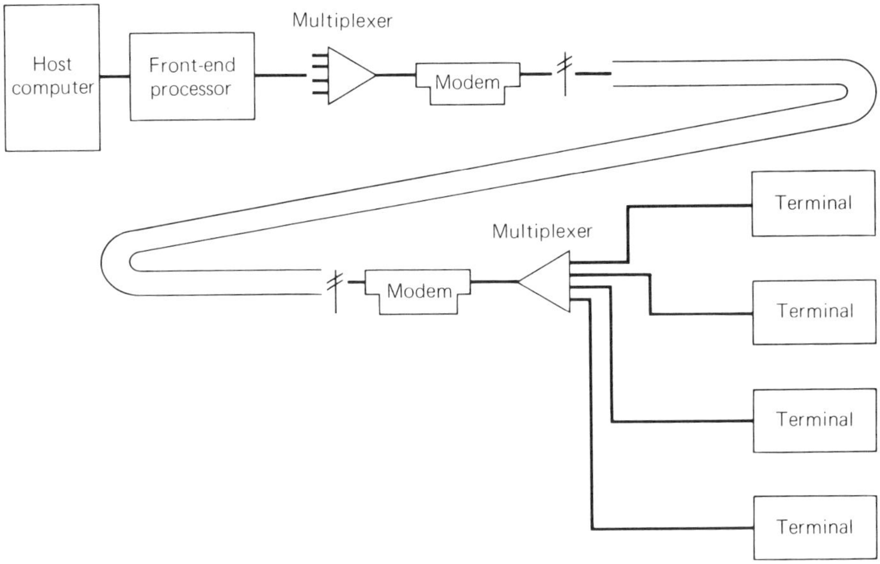

Figure 6.1: Example of multiplexing

ers and the high-capacity data links to the computer. A multiplexer is transparent to the user. The methods of doing multiplexing are covered later in this chapter.

CONCENTRATION. This function serves the same purposes as multiplexing and performs additional functions possible through a programmable device. Essentially, concentration involves taking in several low-speed lines and generates a fewer number of high-speed output lines. Concentration may also involve code checking and conversion, and the reformatting of messages. The process of concentration may also involve the storage of messages until an output slot is available. Concentration is not in general transparent to the user.

There are additional functions that must be performed in a computer network. Some of these functions are implicit in the network components and procedures that follow.

Network Components

Other than computational facilities and file storage normally associated with host processing, a wide variety of building blocks are necessary for synthesizing a computer network. Without going into excessive technical detail, an attempt is made in this section to cover most network components. Because computer networks and distributed systems are rapidly growing areas, new components and concepts are being developed at a fast rate. Therefore, no guarantee is made as to the completeness of the set of components covered.

COMMUNICATION CHANNELS. Communication channels are the circuits used to transfer information from point to point. The physical circuit technology involves metallic conductors and wireless transmission. Included in the former category are twisted-wire pairs, multi-pair cables, coaxial cables, and wave guides. Included in the second category are microwaves with land-based repeaters, satellites, and optical methods. There is currently a considerable amount of interest in satellite-based systems with the primary objective of reducing communication costs. Satellite transmission, however, is not without its disadvantages, a major one of which is propagation delay. The following list gives propagation delay for a coast-to-coast (U.S.A.) transmission:

Route	*Propagation Delay*
Direct line	.016 sec.
Random route	.05 sec.
Via satellite	.25 sec.

The end result of propagation delay is that acknowledgment time is greater so that longer message queues are necessary in the communications software.

FRONT-END PROCESSORS. Front-end processors are used primarily to relieve the host computer from time-consuming communications functions. In systems with a relatively light communications load, the burden of the communications interface can be handled by the host computer. Increasingly, however, communications functions are handled by a front-end processor, which can be nonprogrammable or programmable. Nonprogrammable units are usually called communications controllers or transmission control units that can be used to perform fixed sets of communications functions. There is considerable movement in the computer industry away from nonprogrammable units to full-scale minicomputers that can perform additional computational functions, such as input editing and "standing in" for the host processor in case of failure by maintaining network operation. Fitzgerald and Eason list the range of characteristics and functions of front-end processors as:

1. Connects from one to several hundred communication lines to the main computer.
2. Accepts synchronous, asynchronous, or isochronous, serial or parallel transmission for data coming in from the remote terminal sites.
3. Polls terminals to inquire if they have a message to send or are in a state to receive a message.
4. Handles automatic answering or outward calling on the public switched network in order to connect various terminals to the system.
5. Utilizes a variety of data communication codes whenever a network has many different types of terminals connected to it.

6. Performs circuit or line switching and provides a "store and forward" capability.
7. Handles transmission speed differences.
8. Performs logging of all inbound and outbound messages on a special log.
9. Provides error detection and correction.
10. Adds communication line control codes to outbound messages and deletes these codes from incoming messages.
11. Addresses either a special group of terminals, several terminals at one time, one terminal at a time, or sends a broadcast message simultaneously to all terminals in the system.
12. Assigns serial numbers as well as time and date stamps to all messages that it handles.
13. Is responsible for the "time-out" facility.
14. Performs two levels of editing. In the first level, the front end may add items to a message, reroute the message, or rearrange data for further transmission. In the second level of editing, the front end is programmed to perform specific edits of the different transactions that enter the system.
15. Handles the message priority system.
16. Performs correlations of traffic density and circuit availability.
17. Determines alternative paths over which the data will be transmitted.
18. Performs miscellaneous functions, such as (1) triggering remote alarms if certain parameters are exceeded; (2) performing the multiplexing operations; (3) signaling abnormal occurrences to the cen-

tral computer; and (4) slowing up the input and output of messages when the central computer is overburdened.[1]

It is important to emphasize that a front-end processor is usually configured with its own peripherals and is attached, possibly as an input/output device, to the host system. Through the inherent flexibility of minicomputers, the front-end processor can readily be adjusted to handle future network system modifications.

PORT-SHARING AND LINE-SPLITTING DEVICES. The capacity of a front-end processor is limited to a fixed number of lines called *ports*. When it is desired to increase the number of ports without adding additional front-end capability, a port-sharing device can be used. A port-sharing device is a digital bridge that permits several point-to-point lines to behave as a multipoint line. The limitation of this technique is that only one of the lines involved in the port-sharing can interact with the front-end at a time. A port-sharing device is attached to the system between the front-end processor and its modem. A line splitting device operates as a port-sharing device at the remote end of a communications line. Several terminals are normally connected to a line splitter which is connected to the remote modem. The terminals involved in line splitting are handled as though they were connected through a multipoint line.

[1]Fitzgerald, J. and T.S. Eason, *Fundamentals of Data Communications* (New York: John Wiley and Sons, 1978), pp. 60–62.

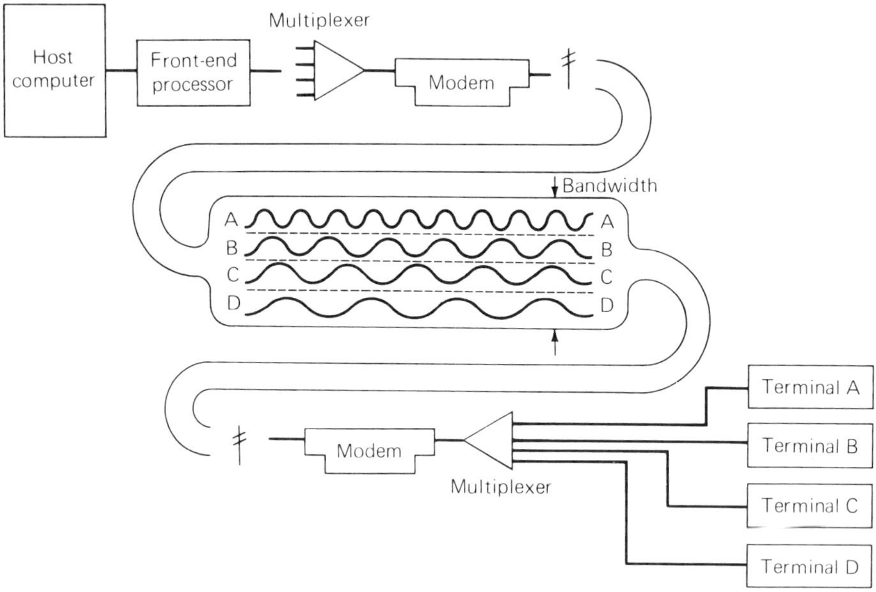

Figure 6.2: Frequency division multiplexing

MODEMS. A modem performs modulation/demodulation, as covered previously, and can have the following characteristics: (1) asynchronous or synchronous, or (2) attached to common carrier line or use acoustic coupling. Asynchronous modems are used for asynchronous transmission and normally use frequency shift modulation for low-speed lines up to 1800 bits per second. Synchronous modems are used for synchronous transmission and normally use frequency or phase shift modulation. Phase shift modulation is customarily used for data rates over 1800 bits per second. An *acoustical coupler* is a device connected to a terminal device that couples acoustically to an ordinary telephone receiver. The acoustical coupler converts digital signals to acoustical tones that are emitted into the telephone mouthpiece. For reception, the acoustical coupler picks up tones from the telephone earpiece and converts them to digital signals. Modems can also be equipped with automatic answer, self-dialing, and equalizing features.

MULTIPLEXERS. A multiplexer combines two or more signals into a single channel and employs one of two techniques: frequency-division multiplexing or time-division multiplexing. In *frequency-division multiplexing,* the frequency spectrum of a data link is divided into subchannels, as conceptualized in Figure 6.2. With this technique, all signals are transmitted simultaneously and need not terminate in the same location. Subchannels can be

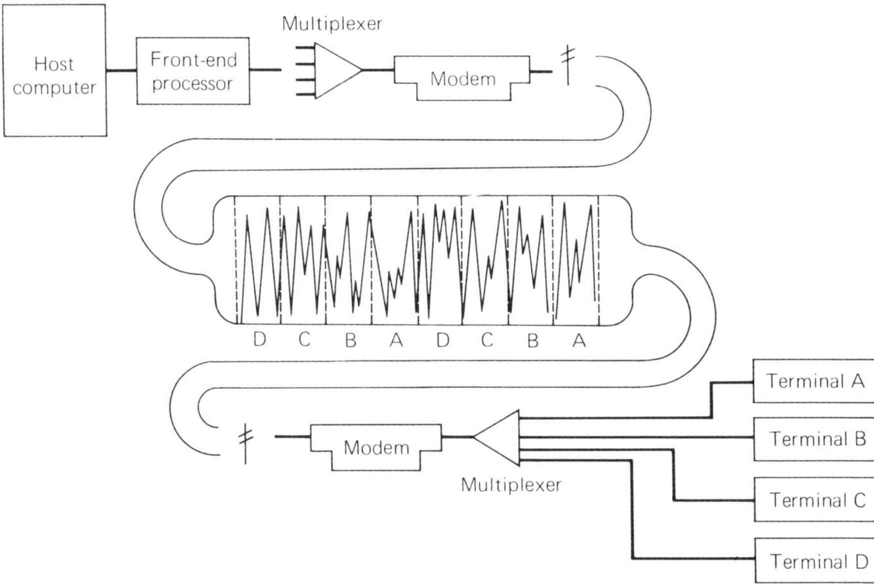

Figure 6.3: Time-division multiplexing

"picked off" at different locations, as in a multipoint connection. In *time-division multiplexing,* bits or characters from several low-speed channels are interleaved and transmitted at a higher data rate, as shown in Figure 6.3. Essentially, the characters are assembled into a frame and transmitted. At the receiving modem, the characters are then disassembled. Time-division multiplexing is more efficient than frequency-division multiplexing but it is costly to have multipoint line drop-offs.

CONCENTRATORS. A concentrator is a programmable processor—usually a minicomputer—that provides adaptive multiplexing. With a multiplexer, the sum total of input and output data rates, at an instant in time, are equal. With a concentrator, a number of input channels share a smaller number of output channels on a demand basis. A concentrator effectively smooths out the traffic in a data link. Because a concentrator normally supports message storage and forwarding functions, local peripheral storage is usually required.

NETWORK PROCESSORS. The term network processor is a general name for a minicomputer that performs one or more of the functions of the following network components: concentrator, multiplexer, front-end processor, polling control station, and the interface message processor commonly used with packet switching systems. In some cases, a network processor is referred to as a *switch,* because it is used for message switching through the handling of multiple inputs and outputs.

Terminals

The computer terminal is the primary device used for communication between a person and a computer or another item of computer equipment. The choice of a terminal is important because it tends to have a long-term effect on the total system. In short, computers are replaced more frequently than terminals. The network and set of computers may be transparent to the terminal operator, but the specific terminal is not. For purposes of description, terminals can be grouped into three classes: batch, interactive, and intelligent.

BATCH TERMINALS. A batch terminal is used for remote job entry and remote job output and consists of an assembly of input/output devices and peripheral equipment. A modern batch terminal is likely to include a minicomputer for control, but earlier batch terminals included hardware control. Typical components in a modern batch terminal are: minicomputer, video display, card reader, line printer, card punch, paper tape device, magnetic tape device, and a disk drive, as depicted in Figure 6.4. A batch terminal is used primarily for high-volume input and output processing and would be connected to a synchronous communications channel. The speed range, determined by the modem, is typically 200 to 9600 bits per second. It is important to note that the remote job entry, remote job output, and synchronous control procedures must be supported by the host computer

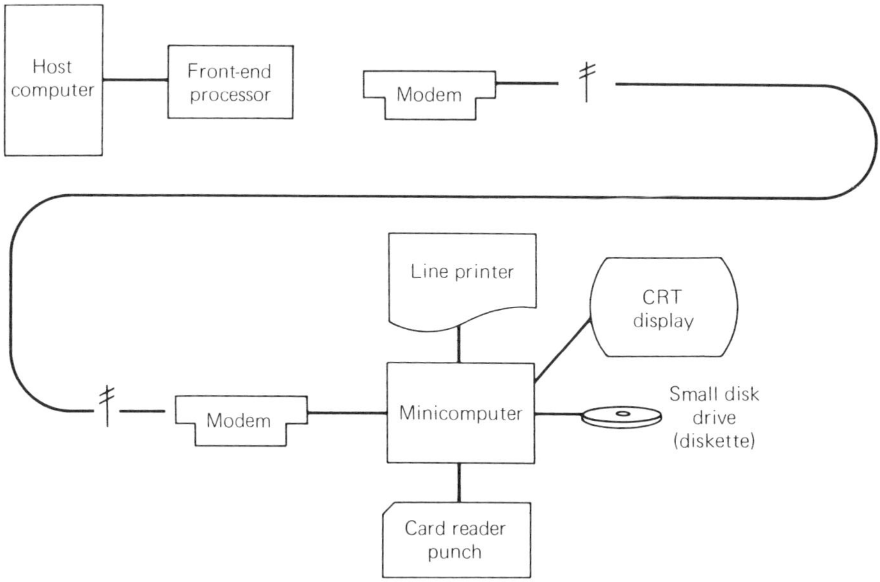

Figure 6.4: Typical RJE/RJO batch terminal

system. A batch terminal contains facilities for buffering input and output to support the synchronous mode of operation.

INTERACTIVE TERMINALS. Interactive terminals are typically used for applications such as time sharing, text editing, interactive problem solving, data entry and message composition, on-line banking, credit reference, reservations, and other types of remote inquiry systems. There are two main categories of interactive terminals: keyboard/printer and video. An interactive terminal typically includes the following components: keyboard, character-by-character printer or CRT display, paper tape reader/punch, and a magnetic tape cassette unit. Figure 6.5 relates the components in an interactive terminal. The data rates with a terminal of this type range from 110 to 9600 bits per second and the asynchronous mode of operation is usually used. (This means that each keystroke causes a character to be transmitted individually, and start/stop bits are required, as covered above.) Interactive terminals are analyzed by considering the type of printing (i.e., solid character, matrix, or nonimpact) and the processing capability (i.e., dumb, smart, local storage, and user-programmable). Haback[2] identifies the various types, as they are listed in Table 6.1, and relates them to a representative set of applications in Table 6.2. Thus, for example, a

[2]Haback, D.H., "As terminal types multiply, so do problems of selection," *Data Communications* 7:7 (July 1978): 58 and 61.

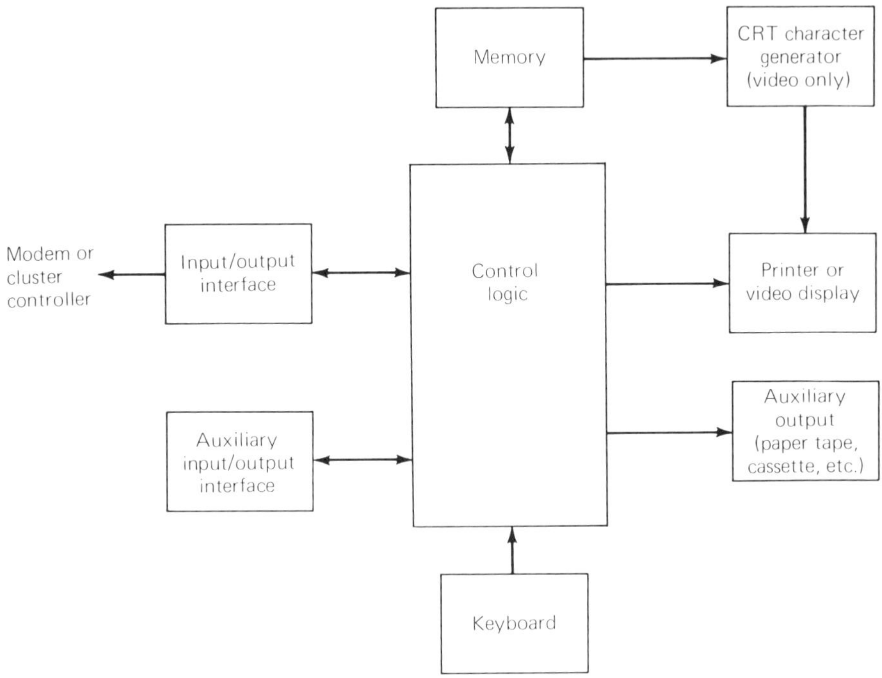

Figure 6.5: Block diagram of interactive terminal

"dumb" terminal with CRT (i.e., type 4) would be appropriate for an inquiry response application. An interactive terminal is usually connected to a modem that is connected to the communications line. In some cases, however, a cluster of video terminals is attached to a "video display control unit," which is connected to the modem. In the latter case, the video display control unit may have a line printer attached to it for hard-copy output.

INTELLIGENT TERMINALS. The term intelligent terminal refers to a terminal with a built-in computer—usually a microcomputer. A synonym for intelligent, in this case, is "smart." A terminal without a built-in computer is sometimes referred to as "dumb." The primary advantage of intelligent terminals is that they can prompt the operator for a sequenced set of input values, and then perform editing, logging, file maintenance, formatting, and communications processing. The same functions, if performed by a host processor, would require an excessive amount of communications and CPU time for several terminals. An intelligent terminal normally consists of a small processor, read-only memory (ROM), main storage or random-access memory (RAM), and a complement of auxiliary devices. The programs needed to drive the terminal are held in ROM, which is nonvolatile.

Table 6.1: Terminal Types

	TELEPRINTER			CRT
	IMPACT			
CATEGORIES	SOLID CHARACTER	MATRIX	NON-IMPACT	
Dumb	1	2	3	4
Smart	5	6	7	8
Local Storage	9	10	11	12
User Programmable	13	14	15	16

Typical processing tasks are communications processing, keyboard read, driving a printer, driving a video display, driving a special display, code conversion, writing a block of data to a diskette or cassette, reading from external storage device, and reading from a special device. The list of special devices includes card readers (of various kinds), magnetic badge readers, scanning wands, optical readers, and electronic scales. Typical applications are data entry, POS service,* transaction processing, graphics, and local processing. In the case of local processing intelligent terminal systems, a local branch in a multibranch business can have control over local data processing. Thus, transactions can be processed or stored locally and access is available to a central system for further processing. While a minicomputer with peripherals would ordinarily be required for local processing, it is perhaps the "minimum" form of distributed processing.

Summary

A computer network performs a set of well-defined functions, uses a set of network components, and adheres to a collection of rules and procedures. Not all network functions are customarily recognized and are identified as host processing, front-end processing, connection, switching and flow control, routing, measurement, polling, conditioning and equalizing, multiplexing and concentration. The network components, other than com-

*The acronym POS originated as a "point-of-sale" device for retail establishments—i.e., cash register-type devices. Since, POS has alternately come to mean "point of service" for financial applications, and "point of use" in general.

Table 6.2: Terminal Applications

APPLICATION	TYPE OF TERMINAL 1	2	3	4	5	6	7	8	9	10	11	12	13	14	15	16
General timesharing	●	●	●	●												
Inquiry response				●												
Data entry								●				●				●
Research lab														●	●	●
Salesman			●													
Text preparation					●				●				●			
Generation of internal reports						●	●			●						
Generation of external documents, forms					●								●			
Access to multiple networks														●		●
Message I/O										●	●					
Program development										●	●	●				
Small system console	●			●												
Data checking/verifying								●								
Small office combined unit*													●			
Personal/hobby		●		●												
Computer-aided instruction		●				●										
Computer-aided design														●		●

*Typing, text-editing, processing

putational facilities and file storage normally associated with host processing, are communication channels, front-end processors, port-sharing and line-splitting devices, modems, multiplexers, concentrators, and network processors. The communication terminal is the primary device used for communication between a person and a computer or another item of computer equipment. Terminals are grouped into three classes for purposes of description: batch, interactive, and intelligent. Collectively, the various classifications include remote job entry/output work stations, keyboard/printer terminals, video displays, data entry devices, POS devices, graphics terminals, and local processing terminals.

7

Network Procedures

A computer network requires a set of rules and procedures for exchanging messages between nodes and a software system for controlling the network components, performing the network functions, and managing message traffic within the network. This chapter gives a brief example of packet switching, an overview of network software, and a summary of network protocols.

Example of a Packet Switching System

In a packet switching system, the messages that pass between interface message processors (IMPs) must have a well-defined structure so that the network components will know what to do with them. Figure 7.1 gives a schematic of a message as it might exist in a computer network. The start of header (SOH), start of text (STX), end of transmission block (ETB), and acknowledge (ACK) are control codes. The header contains control information including the origin and destination of a message. The text is the set of messages, which must be decomposed by the destination computer system. The acknowledge (ACK) code is issued by the receiving computer to acknowledge receipt of a message.

Figure 7.2 contains a schematic of packet switching between host computers. Each packet is placed in the network and is forwarded to successive IMPs until it arrives at the IMP for its destination. At that point, the messages are transmitted to the host computer via a host-to-IMP protocol.

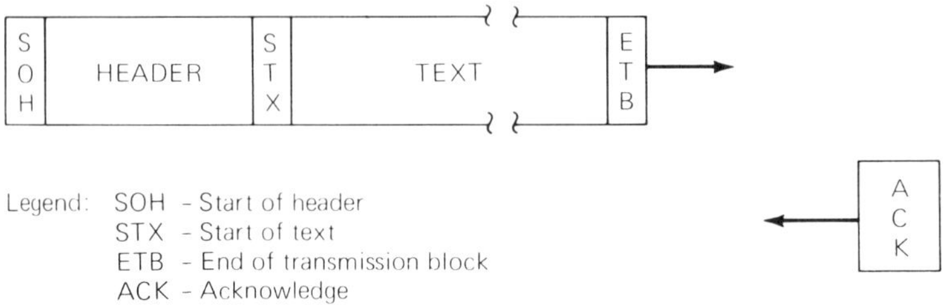

Figure 7.1: Structure of a message in a computer network

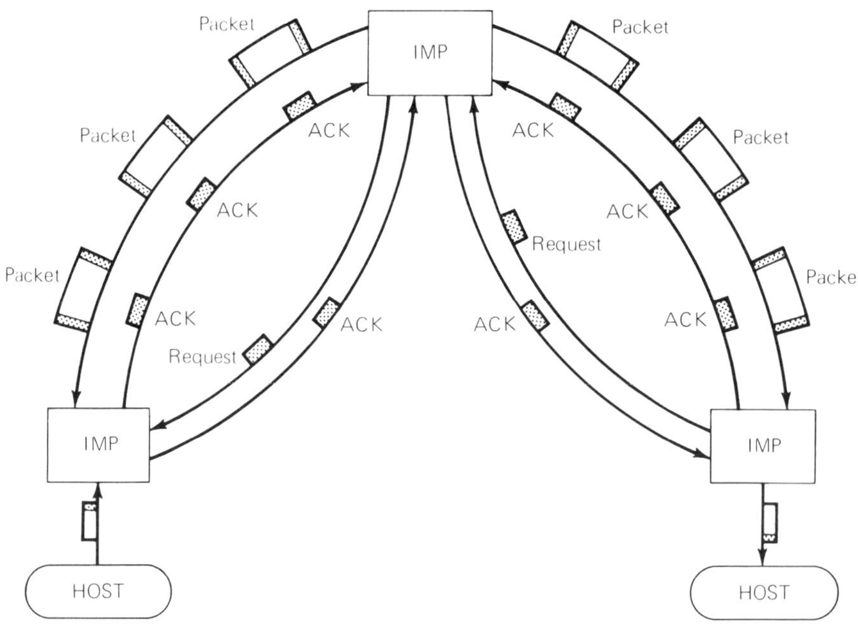

Figure 7.2: Schematic of packet switching between host computers

Communications Software

The objective of communications software is to provide complete control over the network components, but at the same time provide device independence to the application programs. In a communications environment, this means a decreased concern over line control procedures, buffering, and network management in general.

The primary item of communications software is the *network control program* that resides in the host computer system, front-end processor, or network processor and contains software components for performing the following network functions:

1. Data link control
2. Path control
3. Transmission control

Data link control manages the links between nodes in a network. *Path control* routes messages between nodes in a network. *Transmission control* manages the flow of data into and out of the network through the network control program. These functions are reflected in a generalized message structure as shown in Figure 7.3.

The network control program contains three major components:

1. The *input/output device module,* which performs data link control
2. The *line control module,* which performs path control
3. The *network control module,* which performs transmission control

As depicted in Figure 7.4, the network control program also manages queues and buffers, and is thus able to support the various network functions including remote concentration.

Protocols

A protocol is a set of conventions between communicating nodes that governs the format and content of messages to be transmitted. As implied in the preceding section on communications software, it is desirable to have several levels of protocols to facilitate the flow of messages between processes. Thus, a higher-level protocol may use a lower-level protocol. A network frequently used for introducing protocols is the ARPA net-

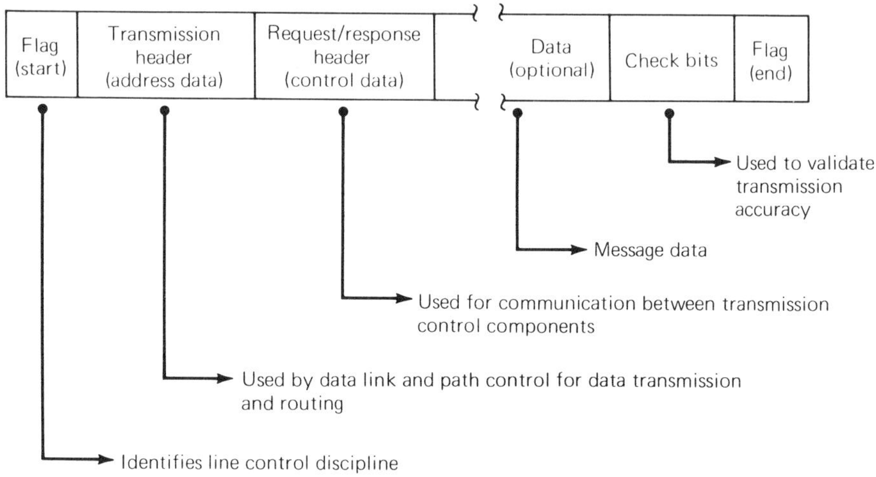

Figure 7.3: Generalized message structure

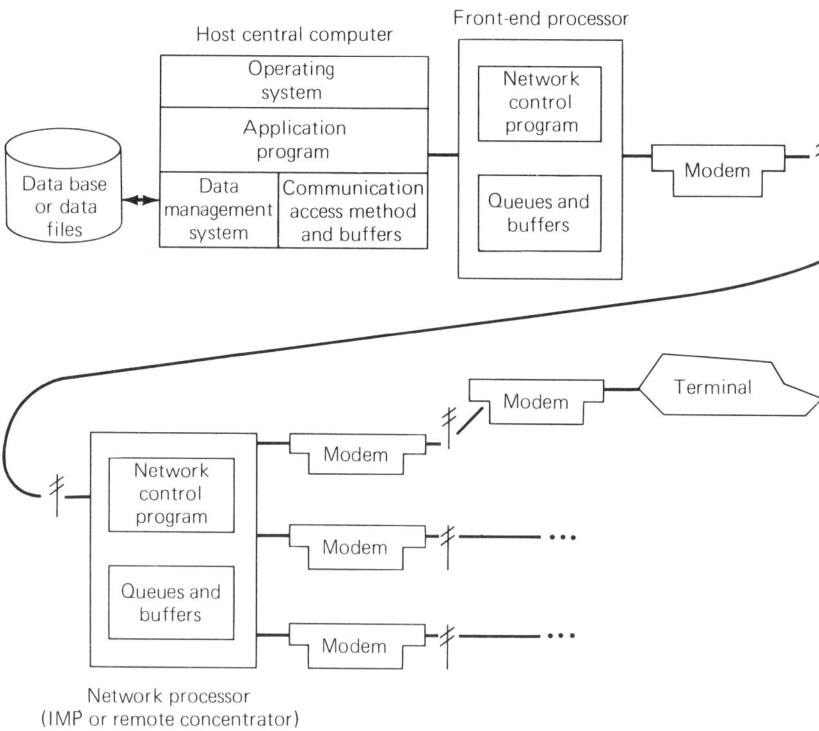

Figure 7.4: Communication software organization

work,* known as ARPANET, composed of a set of host processors, each with its own IMP. In ARPANET, four layers of protocol are identified:

1. *IMP-to-IMP protocol*—permits packet switching between IMPs
2. *IMP-to-host protocol*—permits communication between host computer systems
3. *Host-to-host protocol*—permits communication between processes (i.e., programs) running on different host systems
4. *User-level protocol*—permits users to access host computer systems in the ARPA network

User-level protocols include and encompass the following functions:

1. *Initial connection*—used to initiate a connection to a remote computer system or process
2. *File transfer*—used to transmit files from one host computer system to another
3. *Remote-job-entry*—used to transmit a job to a remote location
4. *Virtual terminal*—used to connect any terminal to any host computer system

While higher-level protocols vary between networks, the lower-level protocols are fairly well established—even though there is a strong tendency for even lower-level protocols to vary among different computer manufacturers. Two of the widest known lower-level protocols were developed by IBM: Binary Synchronous Communications (BSC)

*ARPA stands for Advanced Research Projects Agency.

and Synchronous Data Link Control (SDLC). Both are briefly covered in the following sections.

Binary Synchronous Communications (BSC)

Binary synchronous communications (BSC) is a character-oriented protocol, developed by IBM, which is widely used by the computer communications industry. A schematic of a BSC message is given in Figure 7.5, and the corresponding codes are given in Table 7.1. The optional header field is user defined and it has been used to specify a message number and a device address. The message text is initiated with a STX character and is terminated with a ETX character, after which follows a block check character representing a polynomial check digit.

BSC uses half-duplex transmission and thereby requires a line turnaround and an acknowledgment between blocks. Thus, it is necessary to acknowledge every message transmitted. The header field is not used for control and addressing; special control messages are used for this purpose.

The PAD character is a series of alternating zeros and ones used to facilitate synchronization. The PAD character is followed by two SYN characters to achieve synchronization followed by the block to be transmitted. Thus, a two-message data exchange in BSC might take place as follows:

Activity	*Transmission*
Station sends inquiry message indicating it has data to send	PAD SYN SYN ENQ BCC BCC PAD

Figure 7.5: Schematic of a Binary Synchronous Communications (BSC) message

Table 7.1: Binary Synchronous Communications (BSC) Codes Used in This Section

PAD	—series of alternating 0's and 1's
SYN	—synchronization characters
SOH	—"start of header" character
STX	—"start of text" character
ETX	—"end of text" character
BCC	—block check characters
EOT	—"end of transmission" character
ACK 0	—even positive acknowledgment
ACK 1	—odd positive acknowledgment
NAK	—negative acknowledgment
DLE	—data link escape
ENQ	—inquiry

Activity	*Transmission*
Line turnaround	
Computer responds with positive acknowledgment	PAD SYN SYN ACK ONE BCC BCC PAD
Line turnaround	
Station send first message	PAD SYN SYN STX TEXT ETX BCC BCC PAD
Line turnaround	
Computer responds with positive acknowledgment to first message	PAD SYN SYN ACK ZRO BCC BCC PAD
Line turnaround	
Station sends second message	PAD SYN SYN STX TEXT ETX BCC BCC PAD
Line turnaround	
Computer responds with positive acknowledgment to second message	PAD SYN SYN ACK ONE BCC BCC PAD
Line turnaround	
Station sends "end of transmission"	PAD SYN SYN EOT PAD

SYN	SYN	SOH	COUNT (4 bits)	FLAG (2 bits)	RESPONSE (8 bits)	SEQUENCE (8 bits)	ADDRESS (8 bits)	CRC 1 (16 bits)

MESSAGE	CRC 2 (16 bits)

Figure 7.6: Schematic of a Digital Data Communications Message Protocol (DDCMP) message

A polynomial check value is computed from the characters in the message before the message is transmitted and is inserted in the message as two block check characters (BCCs). On the receiving end, the polynomial check value is again computed. If the values differ, then a negative acknowledgment (NAK) is returned indicating that retransmission should take place.

In transmitting binary data, such as fixed-point or floating-point values, it is possible to inadvertently generate control characters. The *transparent mode* is used to circumvent this situation. In the transparent mode, data that is to be treated as bit patterns is delimited by DLE STX and DLE ETX, as in the following example:

DLE	STX	Any Bit Pattern	DLE	ETX

If the bit pattern corresponding to the DLE code appears in the text, then another DLE character is inserted by the sending station. On the receiving end, the computer deletes one DLE character from each pair of DLE characters.

Use of the binary synchronous communications (BSC) protocol is heavily dependent upon the information codes used (i.e., BCD, ASCII, EBCDIC, etc.) and scanning is required at both ends of a data link. The upshot of the situation was that there was a need to eliminate the dependence of data link control from the information codes.

Another well known character-oriented protocol is Digital Data Communications Messages Protocol (DDCMP) developed by the Digital Equipment Corporation. In DDCMP, the length of a message is contained in a required header field as suggested in Figure 7.6. This feature eliminates the need for the transparent mode in BSC.

Synchronous Data Link Control (SDLC)

Synchronous data link control (SDLC) is a bit-oriented line discipline developed by IBM for synchronous data transmission over half-duplex or duplex lines. SDLC is presented here as being typical of other related line disciplines, such as the following:

ADCCP—Advanced Data Communications Control Procedure developed as an American National Standard
HDLC—High level Data Link Control developed by the International Standards Organization (ISO)
BDLC—Burroughs Data Link Control developed by the Burroughs Corporation
UDLC—Universal Data Link Control developed by Sperry UNIVAC

Some of the objectives in developing an SDLC protocol are that the line discipline should be independent of particular bit patterns and amenable to diverse transmission modes, such as half-duplex, duplex, hub polling, loop configurations, point-to-point, multipoint, leased, and dial-up. The methods are particularly significant from the standpoint of multipoint line capability, since the traffic of the multiple stations on a line must be coordinated. Also, the technique used for terminal addressing must be applicable to and appropriate for every station on a multipoint line.

Some insight into the need for an SDLC type protocol can be derived from a brief presentation of the major types of polling. The most common form of polling is known as "roll call" polling wherein a polling list is used by the control station to sequentially poll the stations on a multipoint line. Because of overhead and line turnaround time, "roll call" polling is inefficient. Two alternatives are to use either a "loop configuration" or "hub polling."

LOOP CONFIGURATION. With a loop configuration, as suggested by Figure 7.7, the control station sends a polling message to the first station in the loop. If it has messages to transmit, then that station sends them to the control station. If the sending station has no messages to transmit or when its transmission has been completed, the polling message is passed to the next station in the loop and the process continues until the entire loop is polled. Messages are passed through the loop with an address header; a station pulls off messages with its own address. This method has a built-in polling sequence, based on loop position. However, the control station may address a particular station with a polling request. For local loop configurations, modems may not be required—as in a retail establishment with POS terminals. A disadvantage to a loop configuration is that they are sensitive to terminal failures, which would make the loop inoperative. This problem can be eliminated through double loops and terminal bypass, which alter the economic advantages of the techniques.

HUB POLLING. With hub polling, sometimes referred to as *hub "go ahead" polling,* each tributary station is connected to the control station and to adjacent stations, as depicted in Figure 7.8, through output and input lines. The control station can transmit messages to any of its tributary stations through the output line. A tributary can transmit messages to the control

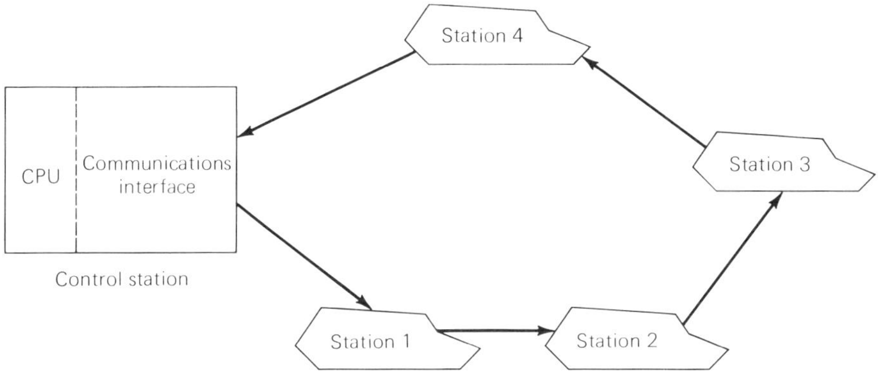

Figure 7.7: Loop configuration

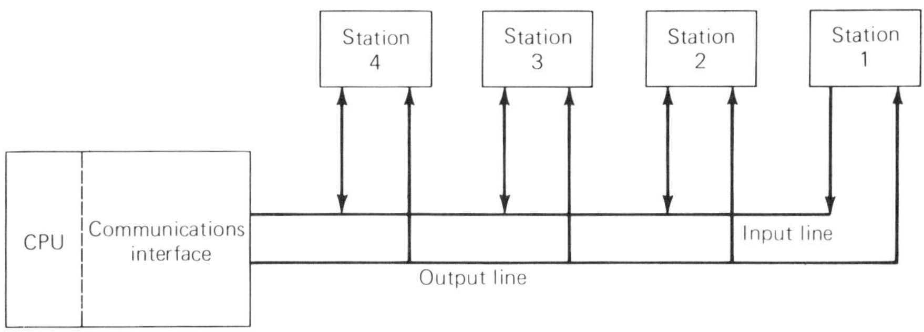

Figure 7.8: Hub polling

station or to the adjacent station through the input line. Hub polling operates as follows. The control station sends a polling message to the most remote station on the multipoint line, e.g., Station 1 in Figure 7.8. That station transmits all of its stored messages to the control station and then passes the polling message to the adjacent station, e.g., Station 2 in Figure 7.8. This station transmits its stored messages to the control station and passes its polling message to the adjacent station, and the process continues until the closest station on the line passes the polling message back to the control station. Then the control station initiates the entire process again by sending the polling message to the most remote station on the multipoint line. One of the advantages of hub polling is that it uses the input line only. Thus, the control station may transmit to any of its tributary stations at any time via the output line.

TERMINOLOGY. In SDLC, each message transmitted is referred to as a *frame* and must adhere to an established format. A *primary station* is

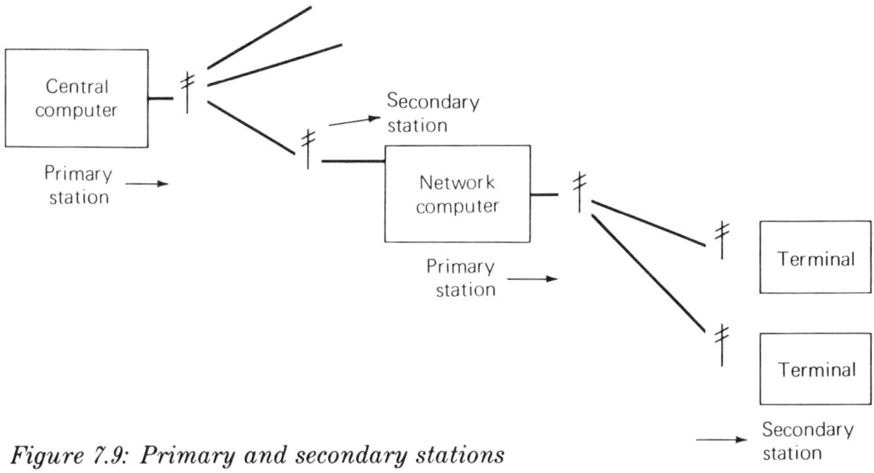

Figure 7.9: Primary and secondary stations

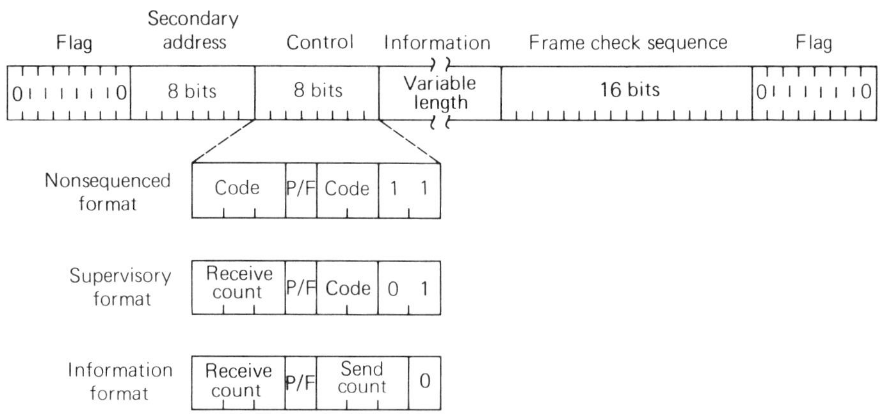

Figure 7.10: SDLC frame

analogous to the control station in multipoint terminology; the *secondary station* is analogous to the tributary station. However, a station can at different times be a primary and a secondary station. Figure 7.9 depicts the concept of primary and secondary stations.

MESSAGE FORMAT. A schematic of an SDLC frame is given in Figure 7.10. It can be viewed conceptually as follows:

[F][A][C][Information][FCS][F]

where:

F = the unique delimiter, called the *flag,* used to synchronize and delimit the message
A = the address field

C = the control field

FCS = the *frame check sequence* used for error detection

The information field is optional, depending upon the control code. The control field is particularly important since it determines the type of message being transmitted.

SEQUENCING. A feature inherent to SDLC is that all information messages need not be ACKed or NACKed, and a set of messages may be acknowledged with a single response. Incorrect messages are resolved through sequencing. The basis of SDLC is that each transmitting station counts and numbers each sequenced frame. This is known as the *send count* (Ns). The receiving station counts each error-free sequenced frame. This is known as the *receive count* (Nr). All frames that have not been confirmed by the receiving station must be retained by the transmitting station, because retransmission may be necessary. Using Figure 7.11 as a conceptual model, sequencing operates as follows:

1. The Nr count is advanced by B when an error-free frame is received. At all times, therefore, Nr should agree with the Ns of the incoming message.
2. If B's Nr does not agree with the Ns in the incoming message, then the incoming frame is out of sequence and B's Nr does not advance.
3. The handling of rejected frames is application dependent.
4. The Nr and Ns fields are each 3 bits in length so the counts can range from 0 to 7. Although the counts may wrap around from 7 to 0, up

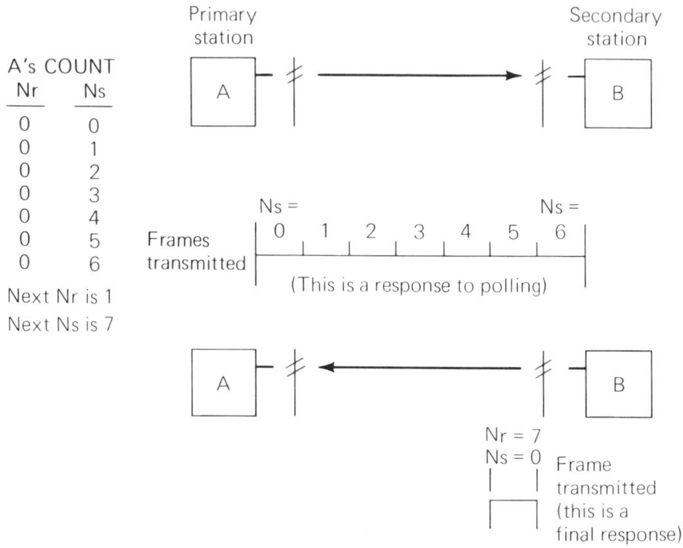

Figure 7.11: SDLC sequencing

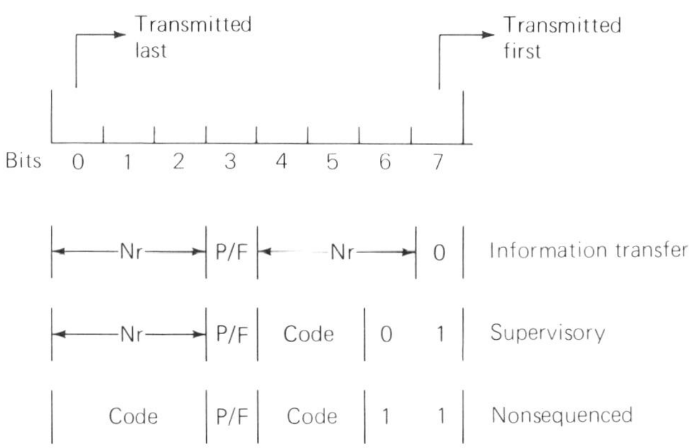

Figure 7.12: Control field format

to seven frames may be transmitted from A to B before an acknowledgment is required.

5. The primary station may initialize the Nr and Ns counts of both stations through appropriate control codes.

Assuming, as shown in Figure 7.11, that station A has sent 7 messages to B, with Ns values ranging from 0 to 6, B may then respond to A with an Nr value of 0 through 7, which would have the following meanings:

B's Nr is	*A's Action*
7 (all messages OK)	A may send frames 7, 0, 1, 2, 3, 4, 5, 6

B's Nr is	*A's Action*
6 (frame 6 in error, frame 6 discarded)	A retransmits 6 and may then send 7, 0, 1, 2, 3, 4, 5,
5 (error in frame 5, frames 5 and 6 discarded)	A retransmits 5 and 6 and may then send 7, 0, 1, 2, 3, 4
4 (error in frame 4, frames 4, 5, and 6 discarded)	A retransmits 4, 5, and 6 and may then send 7, 0, 1, 2, 3
3 (error in frame 3, frames 3–6 discarded)	A retransmits 3, 4, 5, and 6 and may then send 7, 0, 1, 2
2 (error in frame 2, frames 2–6 discarded)	A retransmits 2, 3, 4, 5, and 6 and may then send 7, 0, 1
1 (error in frame 1, frames 1–6 discarded)	A retransmits 1, 2, 3, 4, 5, and 6 and may then send 7, 0
0 (error in frame 0, frames 0–6 discarded)	A retransmits 0, 1, 2, 3, 4, 5, and 6

Through the use of the SDLC sequencing technique, the transmission system will be in the active state a higher percentage of time than with binary synchronous communications (BSC).

CONTROL FIELD. Three formats can be used with the control field: information transfer, supervisory, and nonsequenced. The formats are shown in Figure 7.12; the entire field is transmitted from right to left as indicated. The poll/final (P/F) bit is common and has the following interpretation:

P(Poll)—sent to secondary station to request transmission
F (Final)—returned by secondary station to signal end of transmission

The *information transfer format* contains send and receive counts and is normally followed by the information field. The *supervisory format* is used for polling and to acknowledge transmission and contains a receive count and an appropriate control code. The *nonsequence format* is used for data link management and may optionally contain an information field. Data transmitted via this format is not included in send and receive counts.

INFORMATION FIELD. The information field contains data in 8-bit multiples. No length field is required because the frame check sequence has a fixed length of 16 bits and the message terminates with the unique flag field.

ZERO INSERTION. The flag field consisting of a bit pattern of 01111110 is intended to be unique and delimit SDLC frames. Through zero insertion, the flag field is never transmitted by chance. Before transmission, the sending station inspects the message excluding the flag fields. If five one (1) bits appear in succession, a zero (0) bit is inserted after the fifth one (1) bit. Upon receipt of a message, the receiving station inspects the message for five one (1) bits appearing in succession. If the fifth one (1) bit is followed by a zero bit, then the zero bit is removed. This is the reverse of zero insertion. If the fifth one (1) bit is followed by a one (1) bit, then it is the flag field.

SDLC requires intelligence at both ends of a data link in order to perform the above housekeeping functions.

Summary

A protocol is a set of conventions between communicating nodes that governs the format and content of messages to be transmitted. A packet switching system is a typical example of a case where a protocol would be used. Communications software is designed to provide complete control over the network components and provide device independence to the application programs. The major item in communications software is the network control program and provides facilities for data link control, path control, and transmission control.

Two of the most well-known protocols are Binary Synchronous Data Link Control (BSC) and Synchronous Data Link Control (SDLC). SDLC is typical of several similar systems.

part three

Distributed Systems Concepts

8

Distributed Data Processing Systems

As the scope of computer applications has broadened in modern organizations, there has been an increased involvement of the end user in the control of how the computer is used and in the determination of the systems for which it is used. Certainly, the coming of age of operating systems, data management and data base systems, and communications technology has contributed to this position. However, the upsurge in minicomputers and the availability of application packages have led a movement to put the computer in the hands of the end user. The trend also represents a shift in management philosophy since the dispersion of computing facilities strongly implies a confidence in management control that was previously lacking in the area of data processing. Another important consideration is that many business people feel that with large centralized computer systems, there is a tendency for the "computer to manage them," and the high level of interest in distributed data processing is a direct result of the fact that it provides alternatives that were not previously available.

Technological Advances

The design and development of a distributed data processing system is functionally related to advances in minicomputer technology. A useful analogy using the electric motor by Leo Shpiz of the Digital Equipment Corporation gives some insight into why this is probably true:

> Leo Shpiz, business products line manager, Digital Equipment Corp., provides an analogy using the electric motor. He said before the motor was developed, "factories were designed around the shaft of the water wheel or whatever the

main source of energy was, and not for the most efficient flow of work. The development of relatively small efficient electric motors changed that. Now, we look at the large central computer—it has a lot of power but it is difficult to get at. In the sixties, companies seemed to be designing their organization around the computer instead of in ways which made sense from a pure business point of view.

"The development of the minicomputer-based small business system," Shpiz went on to say, "is changing that in the same way the electric motor changed factory design." He added, "Not that large central power plants aren't needed. Clearly they are, and large central computers are needed also for the kinds of work they do best."[1]

Clearly, when the computer was the primary expense in a data processing installation, the organization was designed around the computer. Facilities and personnel costs were small compared to the cost of the hardware. Through technological advances in the computer industry, hardware costs have been reduced and an increased number of personnel are involved with computers as suggested by Figure 8.1. Hardware costs are no longer the focus of management attention, and organizations can well afford to devote some resources to better utilization of personnel. Since personnel costs now relate to end users, a more optimum placement of hardware facilities would seem to be in order. In short, it is currently feasible to design an information system around the needs of the organization.

[1]Lusa, J.M., "Alive and Well," *Infosystems* (November 1976): 35–38.

Figure 8.1:
Relative costs of personnel, hardware, and miscellaneous items in a modern computer installation

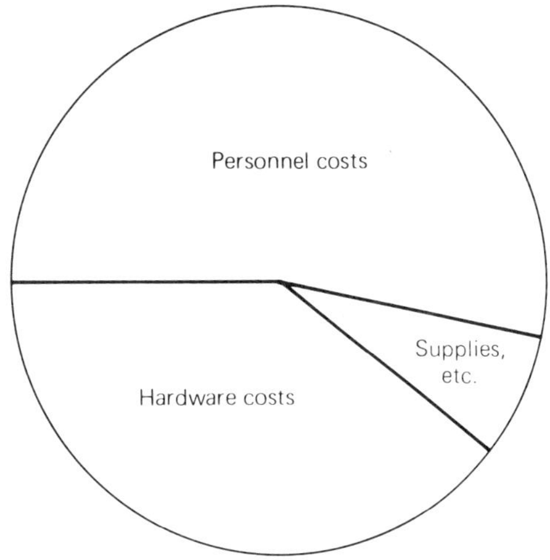

Information Dynamics

In preparation for effective information systems design, it is useful to explore the patterns of information flow in formal organizations.* Using the familiar organization chart, reported information is summarized and abstracted as it flows upward, as suggested in Figure 8.2. As management control information is disseminated, it is expanded and detailed, as suggested in Figure 8.3. In short, information flow is associated with the normal management decision and control activities such that an organizational unit serves as a "pseudo information processor."

The key point to be made here is that because of the reporting and dissemination functions, most information is used locally. Using an 80–20 ratio, 80% of the information used in a department is generated within the department and only 20% comes from outside. Similarly, 80% of the information handled by a department will be used *only* in that department, and 20% will be sent outside that department. Thus, as suggested by Figure 8.4,

*This sequence is based on Digital's *Distributed Systems Handbook*. However, the concepts are established and the reader is also referred to Myers' *The Impact of Computers on Management* and Sanders' *Computers and Management*.

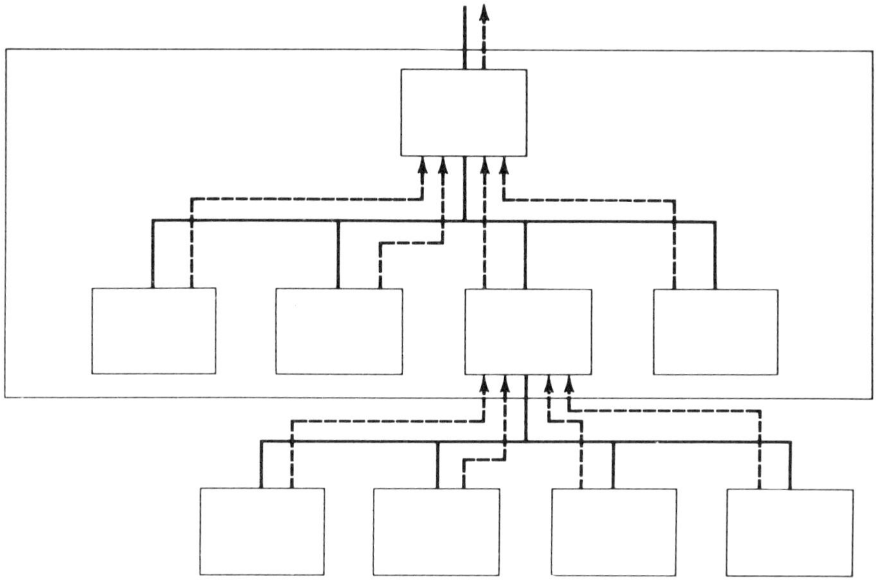

Figure 8.2: Reporting information is summarized and abstracted for management as it flows upward

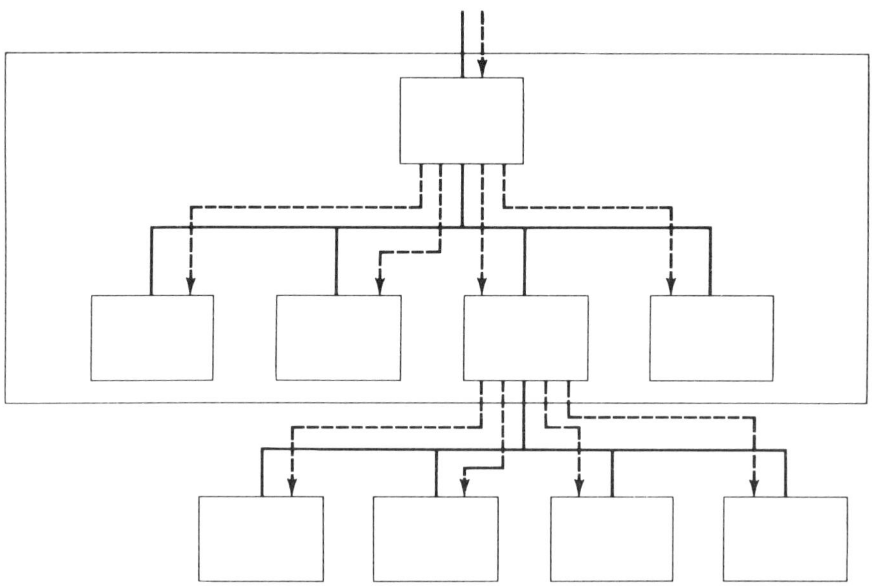

Figure 8.3: Management control information is expanded and detailed as it is disseminated

Figure 8.4:
The value of information to the organization decreases as it gets further from the department where it originated

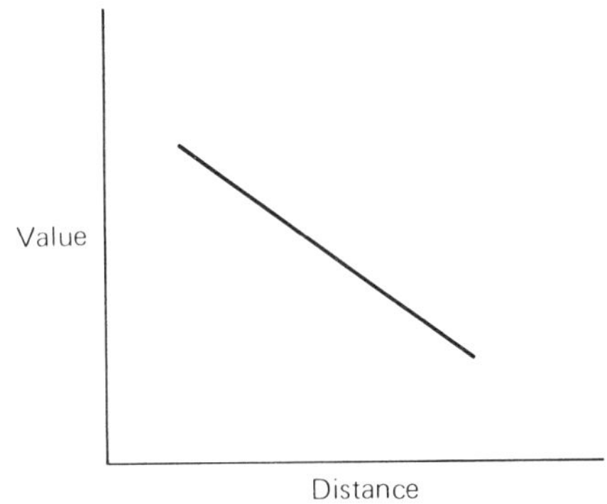

Table 8.1: Grid analysis—one method that can be used for differentiating between local and global needs

	REGION 1	REGION 2	REGION 3	REGION 4
Application 1		X		X
Application 2	X			
Application 3	X	X	X	X
Data base A		X		
Data base B	X	X	X	X
File X		X		X
File Y	X	X	X	X
File Z	X			

the value of information to the organization decreases as it gets further from the department where it originated.

Location of Resources

The situation is clearly one of differentiating local from global needs. One method of making this determination is to use a grid analysis, as shown in Table 8.1. The objective of the analysis is to identify the informational and processing requirements of each location—taken to be either a plant or geographical area. From Table 8.1, it can be seen that application 2 and file

Z are unique in region 1 and could be logically located there. Application 3, data base B, and file Y are shared by all regions and could also be located in region 1 or in a central location established to serve all regions. Application 1 and file X are shared between regions 2 and 4 and would probably be located in either of them or possibly in both locations.

A grid analysis is useful when a pattern exists among the entries in the chart. When a pattern does not exist, then a value judgment or an economic analysis is necessary. In the latter case, hardware and communication costs must be combined with the nonmonetary value of having certain resources in certain locations to determine the optimum deployment of resources.

The trade-offs between data stored locally and globally invariably involve organizational issues. Data stored locally can be managed more informally than if the same data were stored in a central location, and a certain amount of data security is inherent in local storage. Data stored globally is more readily available to the total organization, and less concern over data partitioning is necessary.

Distributable Application Functions

The *effectiveness* of a distributed data processing system is a measure of how closely the design of the distributed system adheres to the informational and processing needs of the organization. Effectiveness is achieved by identifying the application functions to be distributed and integrating those functions in an appropriate total systems design. Three major application functions are recognized: data capture, data processing, and data base management. *Data capture* may incorporate practically any form of input, including data entry, special purpose terminals (such as banking or point of sale), and laboratory data acquisition. *Data processing* may incorporate practically any form of computing and data management, including problem solving, analysis, file processing, reporting, information retrieval or dissemination, control applications, and other financial and record-keeping operations. *Data base management* refers to the use of an integrated set of files and the primary concern is over the manner in which the data base is partitioned. Most other application functions can be absorbed in the above classes.

In a system design, the three major application functions may be established locally, globally, or be nonexistent. The data capture and data base management functions utilize a host processor or incorporate a special processor for that function alone.

Three illustrative examples are considered: an airline reservation system, a banking system, and a retail system. They are intended to demonstrate the manner in which application functions are dispersed in a distributed system. In an airline reservation system, the data processing and data base management application functions are centralized, and, in most cases, the data capture function is also centralized since local processors or intelligent terminals are not commonly used. An airline agent's display/printer is normally driven by the central system. A typical airline reservation system may support from 2000 to 5000 terminals, and concentrators are used to reduce transmission time and support the quick response time

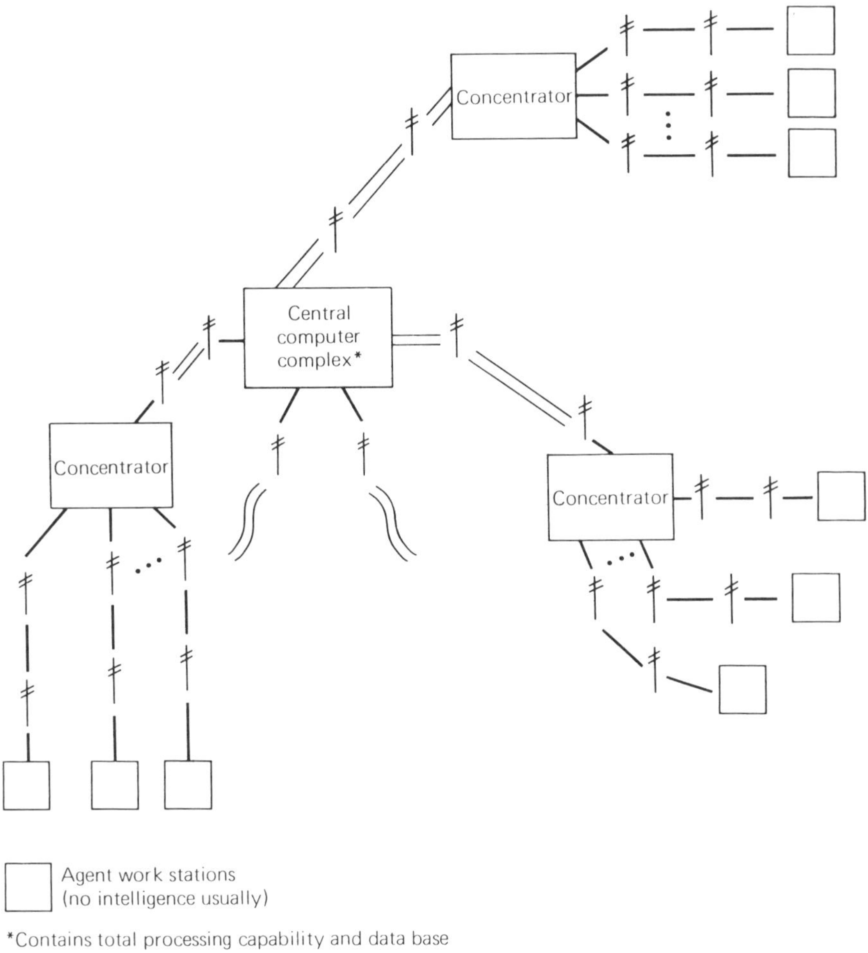

Figure 8.5: Conceptual view of an airline reservation system in which application functions are centralized

required for this type of system. An airline reservation system is conceptualized in Figure 8.5.

In a banking system with transaction terminals in branch offices, the processing is distributed to local intelligent work stations with network computers for polling and for handling local data files normally associated with bookkeeping operations. Because of the need for centralized record keeping associated with the multiplicity of branch offices, the data base management function is centralized to provide global access to all network

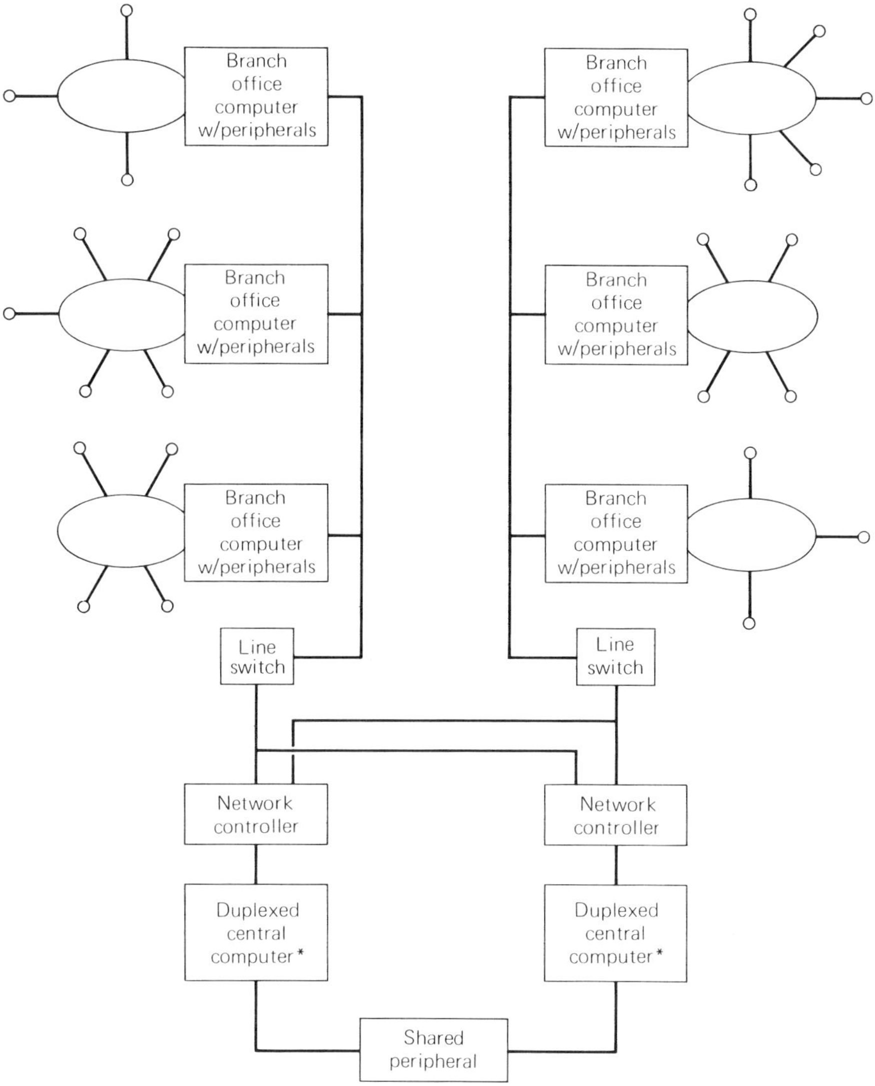

○ - Teller work stations (with intelligence)

*Contains data base processing

Figure 8.6: Conceptual view of a banking system in which processing and data capture are distributed and the data base is centralized

computers. The data base may be referenced on a demand basis during normal banking hours and could be updated during off-hours through a high-speed data collection operation. This type of system is conceptualized in Figure 8.6.

In a retail system with POS terminals in stores, store minicomputers, regional computer complexes, and a centralized computer complex, all three applications functions are distributed, as conceptualized in figures 8.7 and 8.8. In this example, processing is distributed throughout the system and data capture is distributed to the POS devices in retail stores. Several data bases exist. The inventory and credit data bases are centralized, while the accounting data bases are distributed to regional centers. From an operational point of view, the following points can be made:

1. Store management operations are localized.
2. Accounting is handled regionally so that a periodic transmission from retail stores to regional centers is necessary.
3. Regional centers can communicate through a ring structure (or through the central computer complex in the event of a component failure) for transmitting billing data from one region to another.
4. The system demonstrates star, hierarchical, and ring structures.

The retail system is a characteristic example of how a distributed system can closely match a typical organizational structure.

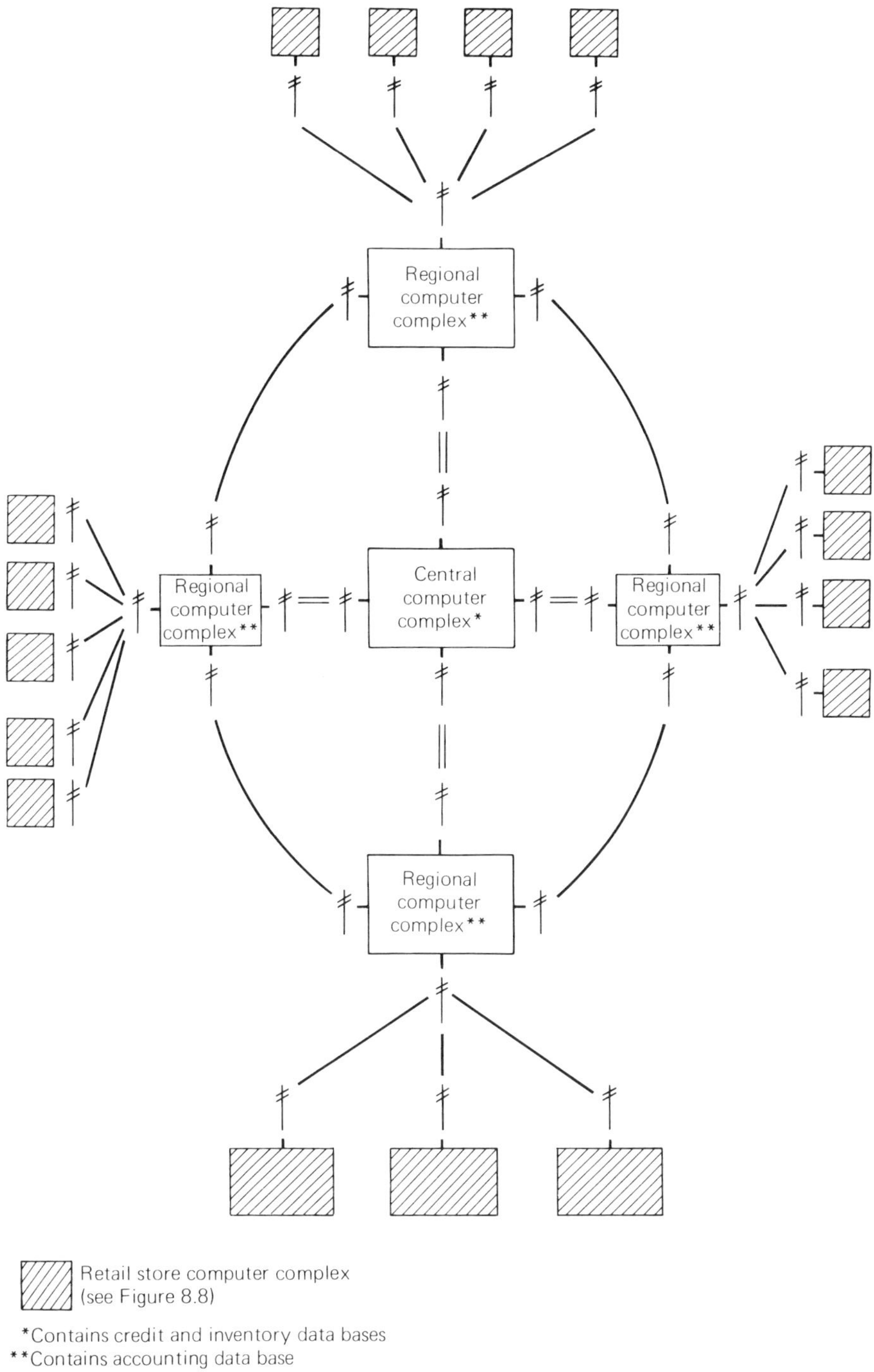

Figure 8.7: Conceptual view of a retail system in which all application functions are distributed

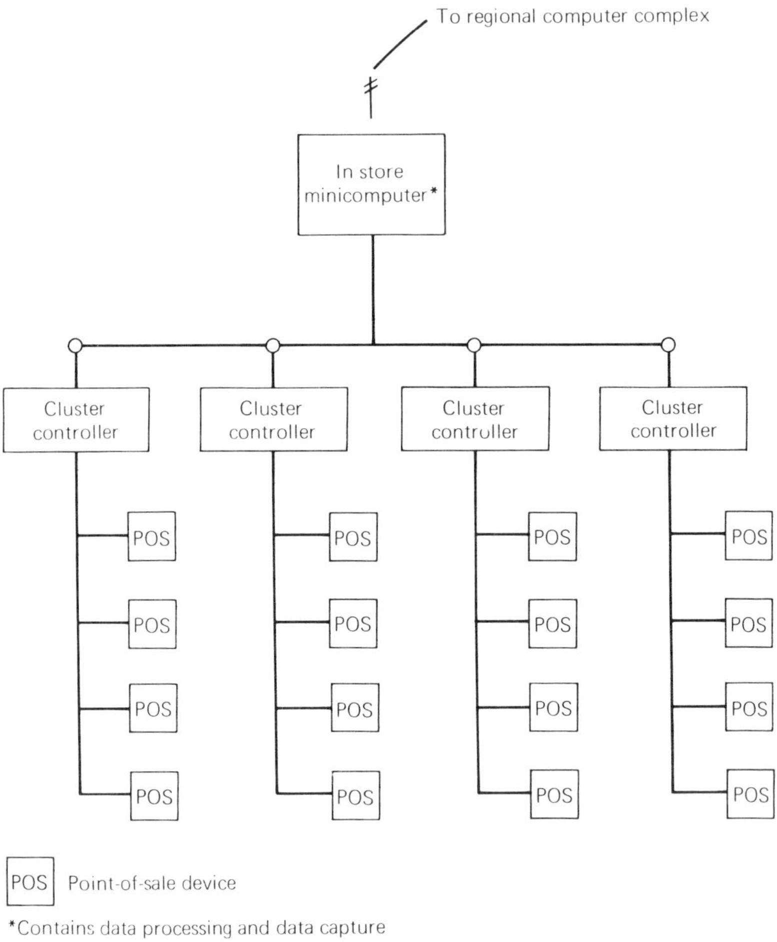

Figure 8.8: Retail store computer complex (this diagram is a logical part of the retail system in Figure 8.7)

Criteria for Distributability

In determining the functions that are distributed in a system design, it is necessary to establish exactly what constitutes a distributed function. Cypser gives the following criteria for a distributed system function:

1. The same function can be executed at more than one node in a network.
2. The function is not completely executable in a single node and

parts of that function are executed cooperatively in separate nodes.[2]

In order for a distributed function to exist, a system resource must be available for executing that function. For distributed data processing, processing capability must be available in a remote location or a means must be available for routing a job to a location with processing capability. For distributed data base management, the data base must be available in a remote location or a means must be available for transmitting data base transactions to the site of the data base system. For data capture, an intelligent terminal device, or data collection, or data acquisition system must exist at the origin of data.

Distributed System Functions

System functions provide the capability for distributing application functions and include such things as operating systems, data management systems, network control programs, and so forth. Through advances in processor technology, system functions can be distributed to practically every node in a network.

Cypser gives the six classes of distributed system functions as:

[2]Cypser, R.J., *Communications Architecture for Distributed Systems* (Reading, Mass.: Addison-Wesley Publishing Company, 1978), p. 72.

1. Management of application processing
2. Management of data
3. Management of communications
4. Application programs
5. Application subsystems
6. Input/output mechanisms[3]

Clearly, processing capability is required for each of the distributed system functions. The *management of application processing* refers to the traditional operating system function which usually incorporates additional capabilities. The *management of data* denotes the data management system associated with or included in most operating systems. The *management of communications* refers to the facility in a node for handling data communications; this facility is commonly known as the network control program. The *application programs,* covered previously, refer to the installation's processing requirements. The *application subsystems* relate to general-purpose software systems that provide a user capability such as remote job entry/output, data base management, or information retrieval/dissemination. *Input/output mechanisms* refer to hardware and software facilities for driving special input/output devices, such as banking cash machines or laboratory interface equipment.

The set of system functions that are present in a given node in a distributed system is dependent upon the applications supported by that node.

[3]Ibid., p. 73.

Each node will possess at least one system function, by definition, and a typical node will probably contain several of them.

The network structure designed into a distributed system will also determine the set of system functions contained in the various nodes. In a system with a fully distributed network structure, for example, there will be a tendency for more nodes, relatively speaking, to include a full complement of systems functions, compared with a logically equivalent system designed with a hierarchical network structure.

Configurations and Partitions

Booth defines distributed processing as "a technique for implementing a single logical set of processing functions across a number of physical devices, so that each performs some part of the total processing required."[4] The various classes of distributed system configurations are known as *partitions.* Five methods of partitioning a distributed system are covered here: horizontal, vertical, geographical, functional, and combinatorial. The classes are not mutually exclusive and are intended to be descriptive of current thinking on the subject.

In a *horizontal partition,* two or more computer systems that are logically equal are connected via telecommunications facilities. In many cases, the computer systems are large-scale information processors supporting local terminal systems. Figure 8.9 depicts a horizontal partition

[4]Booth, G.M., "Distributed information systems," *Proceedings of the 1976 National Computer Conference,* AFIPS volume 45, pp. 789–794.

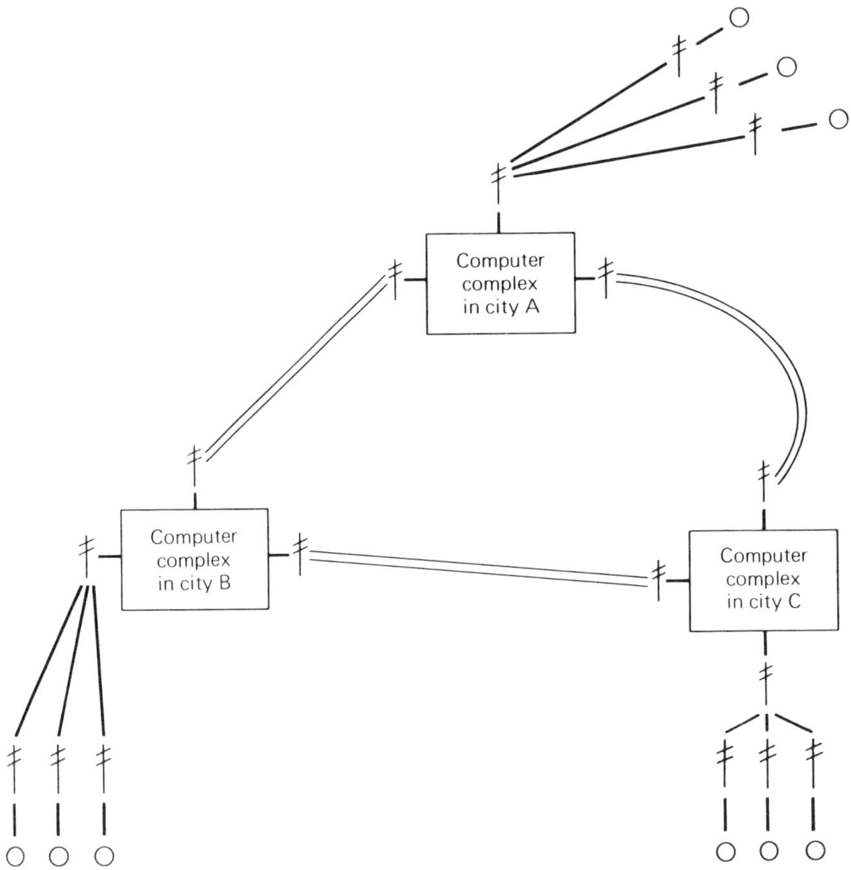

Figure 8.9: Horizontal partition

with computer complexes in three cities. The connection between computing systems is likely to be a high-speed data link for the transmission of jobs, transactions, and data files. Computer complexes in a horizontal partition normally operate autonomously, although in some cases the system configuration is used for load leveling. Most horizontally partitioned systems are a direct result of organizational decentralization.

In a *vertical partition,* data processing is distributed in a hierarchical fashion as depicted in Figure 8.10. (This type of structure is also known as *hierarchically distributed processing.*) The objective in a vertical partition is to off-load processing work to the level in the hierarchy where it is most cost effective. Banking and process control application systems lend themselves to a vertical partition, which may involve distributed data bases as well. The various network computers in a vertical partition may partici-

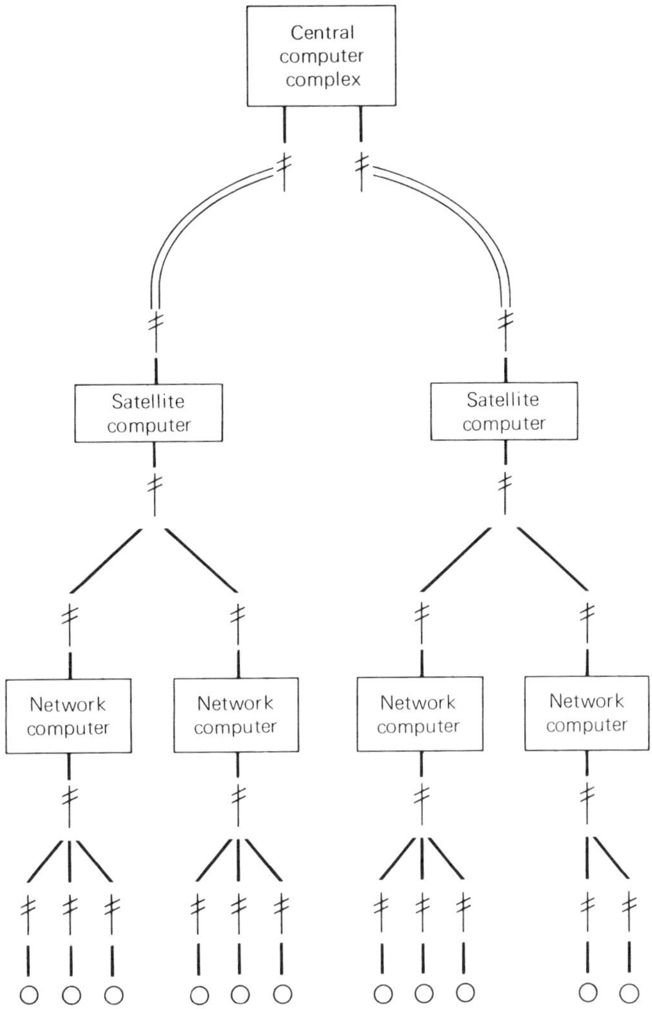

Figure 8.10: Vertical partition (also known as a hierarchical system)

pate in the processing functions or may be used for message switching and concentration, depending upon the level in the hierarchy at which they reside.

In a *geographical partition,* computer complexes are established by geographical location and communicate as in a horizontal partition. Geographical partitions often evolve from previously independent systems that are not logically equal. Consolidation through telecommunications facilities is normally established to satisfy an organization's need for timely information.

In a *functional partition,* a data processing task is decomposed into manageable portions, according to its function, that can be performed in different stages at distinct nodes in a network. This is the "pipeline" approach that takes advantage of the parallelism inherent in many data processing applications. A functional partition may involve file processing or data base operations at various stages in the pipeline, and parallelism may be used when data dependencies do not exist. A functional partition is characterized by the fact that feedback is normally not required. Figure 8.11 depicts a typical pipeline sequence for a retail application in a functionally partitioned system. A functional partition is commonly used with a hierarchical network structure.

The class of *combinational methods* simply gives recognition to the fact that the various methods of distributed system partitioning are commonly used in combination. A typical example is a horizontally partitioned system, established on a geographical basis, in which each computer complex is in itself a vertically partitioned system, perhaps with processing allocated on a functional basis.

Evolution of Distributed Data Processing Systems

As large centralized computer systems become unwieldy and their management becomes more complex, there is an evolutionary trend toward distributed systems. This evolution has taken a characteristic pattern even though most organizations have not progressed past the first stage. The major inducements to move to a distributed system are twofold:

1. Distributed data processing can help to relieve overloading problems at the central facility.

Figure 8.11:
A typical "pipeline" sequence in a functionally partitioned system

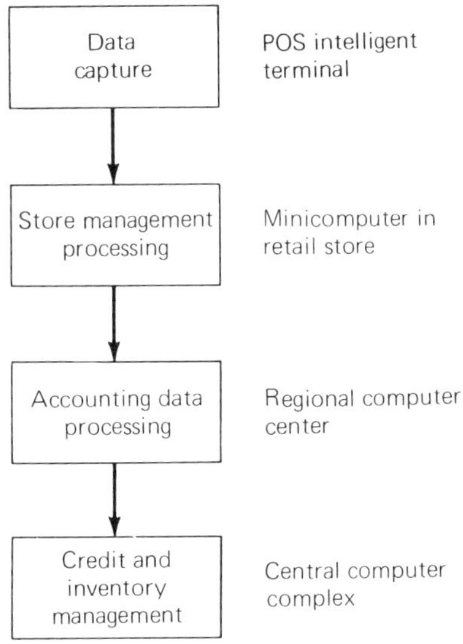

2. Communications costs can be less in a distributed system since summarized data, rather than raw data, is transmitted.

A representative pattern of evolution from a centralized to a distributed data processing system is given as Figure 8.12.

In a simple centralized system with on-line or time-sharing capability, the host computer can and does handle all phases of processing: batch processing, data management, input/output handling, data base management, on-line or time-sharing process, and communications. This kind of system is depicted in Figure 8.12a. Because of software complexity and high supervisor overhead, the system's efficiency is reduced. The first evolutionary step is to attach a front-end processor and remote concentrators to relieve the communications load. The centralized system has evolved to that shown in Figure 8.12b. As the work load increases, one option for avoiding a larger host computer and a possible

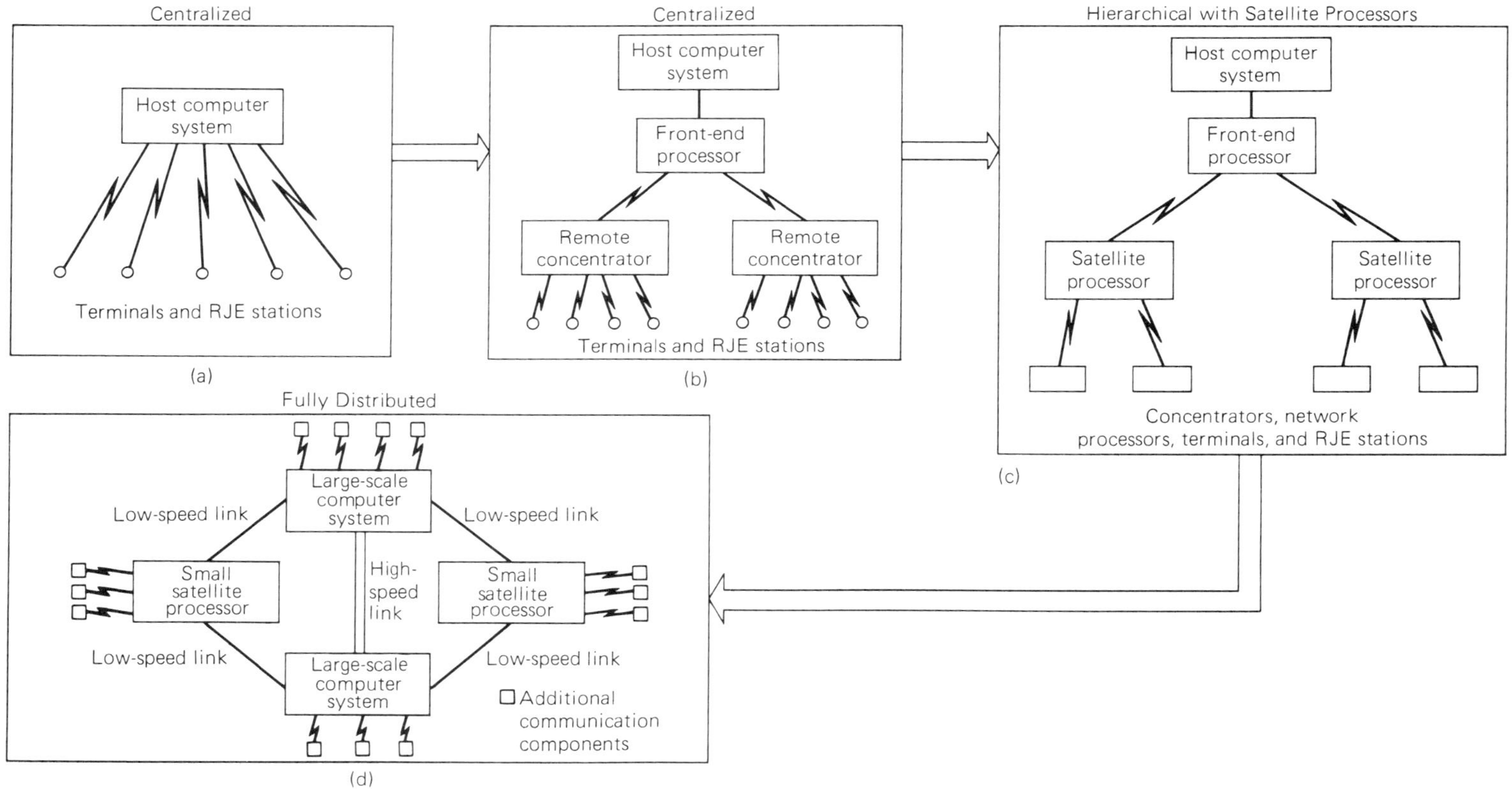

Figure 8.12: Representative pattern of evolution from a centralized to a distributed data processing system

conversion is to off-load certain applications to satellite processors, as shown in Figure 8.12c. Applications that lend themselves to satellite processing are those that are relatively independent of other processing and others that are troublesome because they contribute to poor performance, such as low throughput, slow response time, and so forth. Satellite processing may be obtained with intelligent data capture to further reduce the processing load on the host computer. This is the classical vertically partitioned system.

As satellite processors become increasingly autonomous in operation, applications, and management, there is a tendency to disperse additional processing until the system evolves into a fully distributed system, as shown in Figure 8.12d.

Clearly, in the evolution of a centralized data processing system to a distributed data processing system, the communications resources required to sustain the operation of the system are adjusted accordingly. For example, as the level of dispersion of data processing operations is increased, communications costs are reduced because local computer facilities become more self-sufficient. Lynch has summarized the communications requirements of centralized, satellite, and distributed systems and they are summarized in Table 8.2.[5]

[5]Lynch, A., "Distributed processing solves mainframe problems," *Data Communications* 5: 6 (November/December 1976): 21.

Table 8.2: Communications Requirements

REQUIREMENT	CENTRALIZED	SATELLITE	DISTRIBUTED
Line types	All types, many dedicated	Normally switched	All types, but normally switched
Number of lines	Many	Few	Few
Systems availability requirements	High	Low for free-standing systems	Moderate for free-standing systems
Line costs	Very High	Low	Moderate
Staff requirements	Communications specialists needed (located at central site)	Few if any specialists (satellite sites)	Few if any specialists (remote sites)
Operating system communications overhead	Very high	Small	Small

Summary

Some of the contributing factors to the current movement to put the computer in the hands of the end user through distributed data processing can be listed as follows:

1. Earlier advances in operating systems, data management, data base systems, and data communications
2. Recent developments in minicomputer technology
3. Availability of application packages
4. Shift in management philosophy toward dispersed computing
5. Reduced hardware costs

In short, it is currently feasible to design an information system around the needs of the organization. The patterns of information flow in organizations indicate that most information is generated and used locally, so that the location of resources involves the differentiation of local from global needs. One method of determining the location for resources is to use a grid analysis. An effective distributed data processing system is achieved through the identification of application functions and integrating those functions in a total systems design. Major application functions are data capture, data processing, and data base management. After criteria for distributed system functions are delineated, the six classes of distributed system functions are identified as: management of application processing, management of data, management of communications, application programs, application subsystems, and input/output mechanisms.

A distributed system configuration is known as a partition and five methods are horizontal, vertical, geographical, functional, and combinations thereof. The evolution of a distributed system follows a characteristic pattern; most systems evolve through the following stages: centralized system, satellite system, and distributed system.

9

Distributed Data Base Systems

One of the key resources that must be dispersed in a distributed system is data. A distributed data base system exists when the same groups of data are stored in multiple locations or when data files stored at different locations are interrelated. In a distributed data base system in which all data cannot be supported at all nodes, the decision whether to move data, queries, or programs may be a complex one. There is a general attitude among distributed systems people that the decision should be made dynamically based on data base structure, network composition, communications costs, response time, and the dynamic behavior of the distributed data processing system. Using the total systems approach, the objective of this chapter is to cover the aspects of distributed data base systems that will provide design alternatives to systems designers and organizational management. *In most cases, the topics covered are conceptual, rather than pragmatic, since this aspect of distributed systems is still in the planning stage in most organizations.* Terminology is also a problem, since different terms are used for the same thing and vice versa. An attempt has been made here to preserve the terminology used in the literature rather than add to the confusion by choosing new terms.

Basic Concepts and Definitions

A *data base* is a centralized collection of data stored for use in one or more applications. In most cases, this simply means that the files of an organization are integrated to make better use of the data at a lower storage cost.*

*Lower storage cost may incorporate updating and access operations.

In a data processing application, file definition and access involves the reference to objects and relationships as they exist in the real world through a complex arrangement of data mappings, structural relationships, and complicated graph structures. One way of characterizing a data base is that it is the process of taking the knowledge about data that is implicitly built into programs and making it explicitly available to the user in a formal manner at the systems level.

The structural information about data that is customarily built into computer programs is made available to the user in a data base environment as a set of descriptors. A *schema* is a definition of the data in a data base, and a *subschema* is the definition of that part of the data base that is known to a particular application program. The advantage of the descriptor approach is that the description of the data in a data base exists independently of the data so that relationships between data elements can be changed without requiring changes to the application programs that access them. A *data dictionary/directory* exists in most data base systems as part of the schema to provide a reference to the physical path necessary to access a particular data element.

Components of a Distributed Data Base System

Based on the above concepts and definitions, the three major components of a data base system are listed as follows:

1. *Schema*—this gives the structural information, the format, and the access criteria for the data elements in the data base. (This component also incorporates the subschema.)

2. *Data*—this is the data in the system which may be controlled at the file, record, or field level. (This is referred to later as the *data base.*)
3. *Programs*—these are the programs that access the data base. Since application programs never access the data base directly, the "programs" category includes the applications subsystem and user programs. In this case, the applications subsystem is the data base management system (DBMS).

When the data base system is imbedded in a distributed system and the data is dispersed along with processing and data capture, as covered above, then a network and a communications subsystem are also system components.

Distributed data base systems are classified depending upon the manner in which the above components are organized into a total system.

Distributed Data Base Architecture

The architecture of a distributed data base system is designed around two sets of objectives: data base objectives and communications objectives. *Data base objectives* are to control and effectively use an organization's informational resources through improved availability and integrity of data. Availability, in this context, refers to the accessibility of data by users and may also involve the sharing of data, as well. Integrity refers to the quality, accuracy, and completeness of data. Before the advent of data base systems, the maintaining of availability and integrity was an individual user's responsibility. In a data base environment, this responsibility is borne by the data base management system (DBMS) and the data base administrator (DBA). *Communications objectives* are to minimize the number and size of messages and the length of paths that messages must travel during transmission.

In order to satisfy these objectives, the distributed data base designer has the choice of splitting the data, splitting the directories (and possibly also the schemas and subschemas), and where to locate the data base programs. This section concerns the methods for splitting the data. (The data resources, per se, are referred to here as the "data base.")

In a distributed system, the data base can be centralized, replicated, or partitioned. In a *centralized data base,* the data base resides in a central computer complex. A centralized data base is particularly appropriate for hierarchical network structures in which batch jobs, that do extensive processing against the data base, are transmitted to the central site for processing. For inquiry/response kinds of processing, data can then be transmitted to the remote site on a demand basis.

In a *replicated data base,* all or part of the data base is copied at two or more nodes. Banking is a typical example of where a replicated data base might be used. Each local computer complex maintains a data base of its customer accounts. Before the banking day begins, the local data base is transmitted from the central site. During the day, on-line activity is posted to the local data base. At the close of the banking day, the transactions are consolidated and used to update the central data base. Updated versions of local data bases are then created in the central computer complex and the cycle is repeated the next day.

In a *partitioned data base,* the data resources exist as separate logical segments that are dispersed among multiple computer systems. In most

Table 9.1: Advantages and Disadvantages of Data Base Distribution Methods

TYPE OF DISTRIBUTION	ADVANTAGES	DISADVANTAGES
Common data base accessed by all processors. (Centralized)	No duplication of data, little reorganization required.	Contention among multiple processors attempting to access data simultaneously. Data base is large, so response time is slow. During disk failures, all processors lose access to data.
Copy of the common central data base stored at each processor. (Replicated)	Each processor has access to data base without contention. Fast response time. During failure, new copy can be obtained.	High storage cost due to extensive duplication of data. Updates of one copy must subsequently be made on all other copies. High data base reorganization costs.
Individual data base for each processor in the ring. (Partitioned)	No duplication of data minimizes storage cost. Size of data base determined by application of node, not total corporate requirement. Fast response time.	Ad hoc or management reports must be obtained from different data bases.

cases, the data base is not created as a consolidated unit and then divided into partitions. Rather, it results from distinct data bases that logically evolve into a single data base. Thus, a partitioned data base lends itself to a distributed data processing system with a horizontal, geographical, or functional partition.* In general, there is no duplication of data among the segments of a partitioned data base. As with distributed data processing

*Again, it is recognized that the classes are not mutually exclusive.

systems, a partitioned data base can be divided horizontally, vertically (i.e., with a hierarchical structure), geographically, or functionally.

The advantages and disadvantages of various data base distribution methods are summarized by Lynch[1] and are listed in Table 9.1.

Directory Location

Regardless of the architecture of the data base, the data base management system program that handles a data base transaction requires knowledge of where a physical record is located. This information is contained in the directory. In a system that is not distributed, the data base and the directory reside in the same computer complex. Thus, both components are centralized. In a distributed system, the location of the directory component is a design factor that can affect system loading, availability, volume of communications, response time, and overall system complexity.

Three directory locations are identified: centralized, distributed, and local. With a *centralized directory location,* the directory for the complete data base—regardless of the level of distribution—is located in one computer complex. Subsets of the directory may be placed at local computer centers for segments of the data base stored locally. With a *distributed directory location,* the entire directory for the complete data base is stored at each local computer center. With a *local directory location,* the portion of the directory associated with the local data base is stored in the

[1]Lynch, A., "Distributed processing solves mainframe problems," *Data Communications* 5: 6 (November/December 1976): p. 22.

local computer complex; however, that portion of the directory is not stored in any other computer installation.

A characteristic pattern seems to exist, since directories need to be updated in the same manner that the data base is updated. In the cases of a distributed directory and the centralized directory with local subsets, the local directory can be updated on a dynamic basis. Then during off hours, the local and centralized directories can be conciliated.

OBJECTIVES, OPTIONS, AND COST. The objectives of placing a directory in a particular location are to minimize storage costs, processing time, and communications costs. However, additional options exist. The schema can be placed in one location and the subschema can reside in another location. For certain network configurations, splitting the schemas and subschemas may reduce the number and volume of messages, improve the response time, and help to balance the processing load. This topic is covered briefly in a subsequent section.

Clearly, the amount of storage required for the directory is directly proportional to the number of entries. The local directory method is the most efficient from the standpoint of the amount of required storage since each entry in the directory is stored only once. The distributed directory method, because of the fact that a copy of the complete directory resides at each local computer center, is the least efficient, costing about n times the amount of the local method. (Here, n is the total number of computer complexes, both centralized and local.) The centralized directory location would cost twice as much as the local method if each directory were replicated once. The efficiency of the centralized method would fall somewhere between the other methods as demonstrated by the following inequality where C is cost and $n > 2$:

$$C_{local} \leq C_{centralized} < C_{distributed}$$

Operation of a Distributed Data Base System

Each method of locating the data base and the directory has advantages and disadvantages relative to the operation of the distributed data base system. In fact, some distributed data base system configurations may require additional distributed data base components for their implementation.

Bray lists four alternatives for distributing the data base and the directory:

1. Centralized directory—centralized data base
2. Centralized directory—distributed data base
3. Dispersed directory—decentralized data base
4. Dispersed directory—distributed data base[2]

For some of the alternatives, subcategories may exist. A distributed data base may be replicated or partitioned, for example, and a dispersed directory may be distributed or local.

[2]Bray, O.H., "Distributed Database Design Considerations," in *Distributed Processing Tutorial,* edited by Liebowitz and Carson (New York: IEEE, 1977), p. 8–14.

STRUCTURAL COMPONENTS. Two additional components may be required to sustain the operation of a distributed data base system: a network schema and a switching schema. Clearly, these components may not be necessary for each of the above alternatives. A *network schema* is a representation of the topology of the network. Essentially, it is an interconnection matrix that is used by the communications component to route a message through the network. A *switching schema* is a data base management system component that gives a file or data name and its network location. A switching schema does not eliminate the need for schemas and subschemas, which give additional information, such as data type, size, access controls, and security profiles. A switching schema is used by the data base management system for determining where a nonlocal data element is located in the network.

NODE CLASSIFICATION. In order to effectively route messages through a distributed system, it is important to distinguish between the location that needs to have a service performed and the location that actually performs the servicing task. Bray identifies three types of nodes: requesting, responding, and central.[3] The *requesting node* is the location at which the user makes a request to the data base management system in the form of a data request or the initiation of program execution, as in the form of a batch or background job. The *responding node* is the location that contains the data necessary to perform the task required by the requesting node. Note, however, that the responding node may not necessarily be the node

[3]Ibid., p. 8–15.

at which computer processing is performed or at which the directory is stored. The *central node* is a centralized data store when the data base is organized in this fashion. Note also that the network structure need not necessarily be centralized to support a centralized data base.

TRANSACTIONS. A request to the data base management system can take one of the following forms:

1. An *inquiry*. This type of request does not update the directory or the data base. Processing is required for accessing the directory and the data base.
2. An *update*. This type of request changes the data base but does not necessarily require that the contents of the directory be modified. Processing is required for accessing the directory and the data base and for performing the update operation.
3. A *creation* or *deletion*. This type of request changes the directory and the data base. Processing is required for accessing the directory, changing the contents of the directory, and changing the contents of the data base.

The above requests do not imply data base reorganization, as when fields are added to records in existing files. Creation and deletion operations involve manipulation of entire records, and the update operation involves changing fields within existing records.

CENTRALIZED DIRECTORY-CENTRALIZED DATA BASE. In this configuration, the responding node and the central node are the same. Storage costs are at the minimum level when no dispersed subsets of the centralized directory exist. When the requesting node and the responding node are the same, then communication costs are also at a minimum level. When the requesting node is remote from the responding node, then simple queries, updates, additions, and deletions can be handled as messages and a single transmission, as required, can result in a change to both the data base and the directory. When extensive processing against the data base is necessary, as in a data processing application, then the job should be transmitted to the central site for processing or the file should be transferred to the local computer for updating and then be transferred back to the data base at a later time after local processing has been completed. It is important to emphasize in the latter case that only a file and not the entire data base is transferred between the central and local nodes.

CENTRALIZED DIRECTORY-DISTRIBUTED DATA BASE. In this configuration, it is logically possible but very unlikely that a distributed data base will exist without a dispersed directory—at least for local data. If the local data base were without a directory, then a message would have to be transmitted to a central node to determine a local file or data element location. This would incur communications costs for simple data base requests and would practically prohibit extensive data processing against the local data base. Therefore, it is assumed that if a local node contains a data base, it at least also contains a corresponding directory. If the requesting and responding nodes are the same, then single data requests and extensive processing against the data base would incur minimum communications costs and the level of storage costs would be dependent upon whether the data base were replicated or partitioned. If it were determined through the centralized directory or its dispersed subset that the responding node were different from the requesting node, then either the directory or the switching schema would be used to locate the required node in the network. Simple data requests would be handled as messages and a single transmission could result in a change to both the directory and the data base. For extensive processing against the data base, either the job would have to be transmitted to the responding node or the file would have to be transmitted to the requesting node. However, the centralized directory would require that messages be sent to the central node and to the nodes of all applicable subsets for directory changes resulting from record insertions and deletions. Thus, at least one message would be required for the centralized directory and one message would be required for each of its subsets.

DISPERSED DIRECTORY-CENTRALIZED DATA BASE. With a dispersed directory, the amount of necessary communications would be dependent upon whether the directory were distributed or local. With a distributed directory, a data request for a specific record or field from the centralized data base could be established locally thereby reducing the need for data base management system support at the centralized data base. With a local directory, either of two possibilities exist:

1. The data reference is in the directory. In this case, the data request for a specific record or field from the centralized data base can be established locally, as covered above.

2. The data reference is not in the directory. In this case, the switching schema, if present, could be accessed to determine the location of the node with a directory entry for the data reference. Otherwise, a data request would have to be broadcast to the entire system.

Actually, a local directory and a centralized data base exist as a cumbersome combination and are not a feasible combination from an operational point of view. While a centralized data base with either a centralized or distributed directory location may be feasible for single data requests, extensive processing against the data base would require an excessive amount of communications traffic since requesting and responding nodes are different. In the case of extensive processing, the job would have to be transmitted to the central node for processing or the file would have to be transferred to the requesting node for processing and later be conciliated with the centralized data base.

DISPERSED DIRECTORY-DISTRIBUTED DATA BASE. Four combinations exist: replicated data base-distributed directory, replicated data base-local directory, partitioned data base-distributed directory, and partitioned data base-local directory. The combination of a replicated data base and a distributed directory is classed as not feasible since storage costs are at a maximum level and each directory change and data base update would have to be dispersed throughout the network, resulting in excessive communications costs. The combination of a replicated data base and a local directory is also classed as not feasible since updates to multiple data bases would have to be made and communications costs would be high for nonlocal data references. (This case also includes the combination of a centralized data base and a local directory as a subset.) The combination of a partitioned data base and a distributed directory is classed as a feasible combination because, primarily, the directory is coresident with its data base and would satisfy local information needs with a minimum of communications costs. Thus, in a high percentage of cases, the requesting and responding nodes are the same. The main disadvantage of this combination is that a directory change would require that the change be broadcast throughout the network. The final combination of a partitioned data base and a local directory is optimum because storage and communication costs are minimized and response time is as low as it can be because requesting and responding nodes are the same. For data references not in the directory, a switching schema can be used. Since data needed locally is stored locally, the cases wherein a job requires expensive processing against a nonlocal data base would be minimal and could be handled by the procedures given previously.

SUMMARY OF DISTRIBUTED DATA BASE OPERATION. In the preceding discussion, two combinations of data base distribution and directory location possess the most desirable characteristic from a systems point of view: (1) centralized data base with a centralized directory, and (2) partitioned data base with a local directory. (The characteristics of various combinations of data base distribution and directory location are summarized in Table 9.2.) The two "best" combinations have several common attributes:

Table 9.2: Characteristics of Various Combinations of Data Base Distribution and Directory Location

DATA BASE DISTRIBUTION	DIRECTORY LOCATION		
	CENTRALIZED	DISTRIBUTED	LOCAL
Centralized	Feasible combination. Minimum storage.[1] Moderate communications.[2]	Feasible combination. Moderate storage.[6] Moderate communications.[2]	Not a feasible combination.
Replicated	Feasible combination. Moderate storage.[3] Moderate communications.[4]	Not a feasible combination	Not a feasible combination.
Partitioned	Feasible combination. Moderate storage.[1] Moderate communications.[5]	Feasible combination. Moderate storage.[6] Moderate communications.[5]	Feasible combination. Minimum storage.[7] Minimum communications.[8]

[1]Depending upon the number of dispersed subsets of the directory.
[2]Depending upon data requests and processing against the data base.
[3]Depending upon the number of dispersed subsets of the directory and the number of existing copies of the data base, in whole or in part.
[4]Depending upon whether requesting and responding nodes are the same.
[5]Depending upon whether requesting and responding nodes are the same and whether directory changes are required.
[6]Depending upon the number of complete copies of the directory.
[7]Because the data base and directory are partitioned with no duplications.
[8]Because data bases needed locally are stored locally.

1. The directory is stored with its data base.
2. The combinations correspond to hierarchical (i.e., star) and distributed network structures, respectively.
3. Each combination minimizes storage, communications, or both.

Moreover, the centralized data base with a centralized directory corresponds to the information dynamics in a centralized organization structure and the partitioned data base with a local directory corresponds to the information dynamics in a decentralized organization structure.

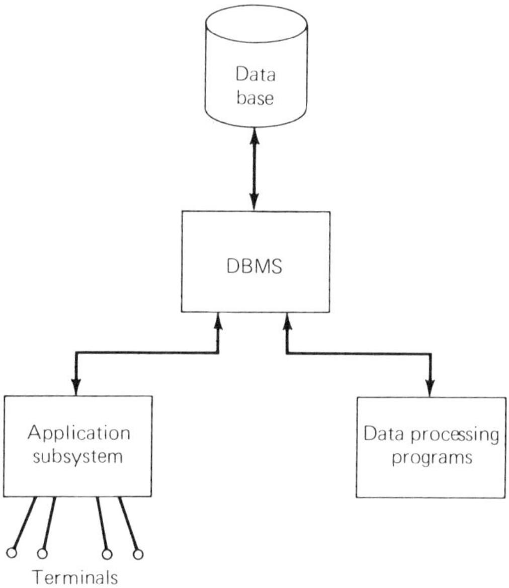

Figure 9.1: Conceptual diagram of a conventional data base system

Network and Data Base System Structures

The application subsystem used to access a data base is commonly known as a *data base management system* (DBMS). As mentioned previously, a user program never references the data base directly but uses the DBMS which does the accessing and mapping of data. Normally, a data base and a DBMS go together in the sense that the file design, file integration, accessing, and mapping functions are interrelated. Thus, a conventional data base system is conceptualized in Figure 9.1. A user can interface with the system through a host language, such as COBOL, for the execution of data processing programs or through an application subsystem for performing on-line data requests. This is essentially a nondistributed means of viewing a data base system.

In a distributed (or network) environment, the network can be introduced in either of two ways: (1) between the user and the DBMS or (2) between the DBMS and the data base. Both methods are conceptualized in Figure 9.2. When the network is introduced between the user and the DBMS, the DBMS is shared among network nodes and/or users and the DBMS is closely linked to the data base. (Recalling the previous section on

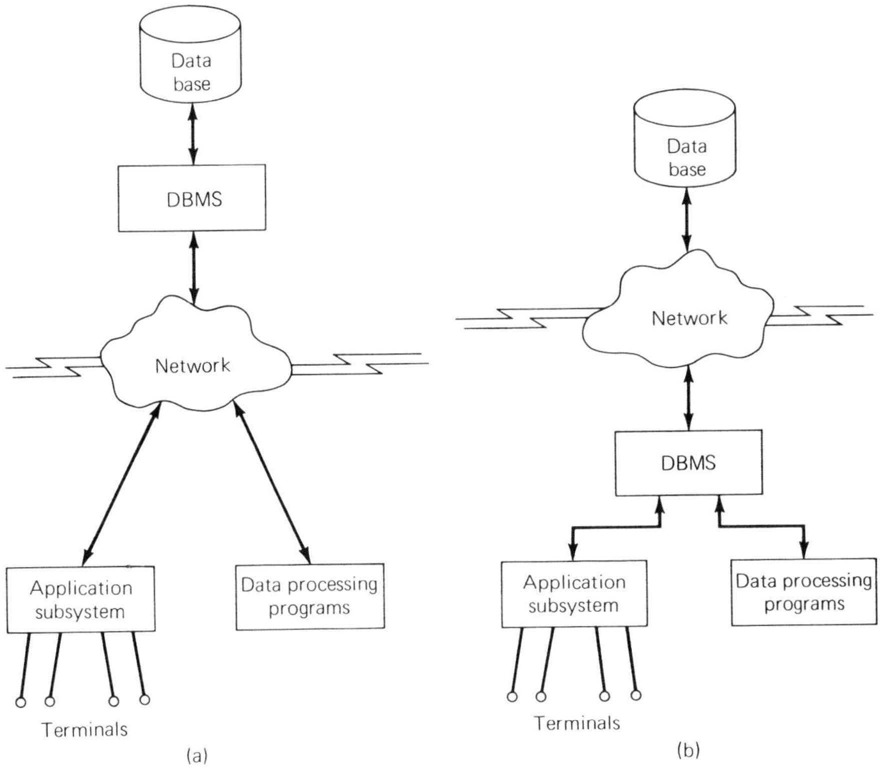

Figure 9.2: In a distributed environment, a network can be introduced between the DBMS (a) or between the DBMS and the data base (b)

distributed data base system operation, this is clearly the case in which the directory reflects the contents of the local data base.) When the network is introduced between the DBMS and the data base, the data is shared among DBMSs in the network and their respective users. (This is essentially the case where the directory and the data base are in different nodes in the network.) *It is important to emphasize that in each of the above methods, computing capability is necessary at both the requesting and responding nodes.*

The significance of the two approaches lies in the type of messages that are transmitted. A simple data query is used as a model. When the network is introduced between the user and the DBMS, then the query takes the form of a conventional DBMS data request to the responding node. The DBMS in the responding node does the mapping and file access and subsequently returns the desired data to the requesting node. When the network is introduced between the DBMS and the data base, then the DBMS in the

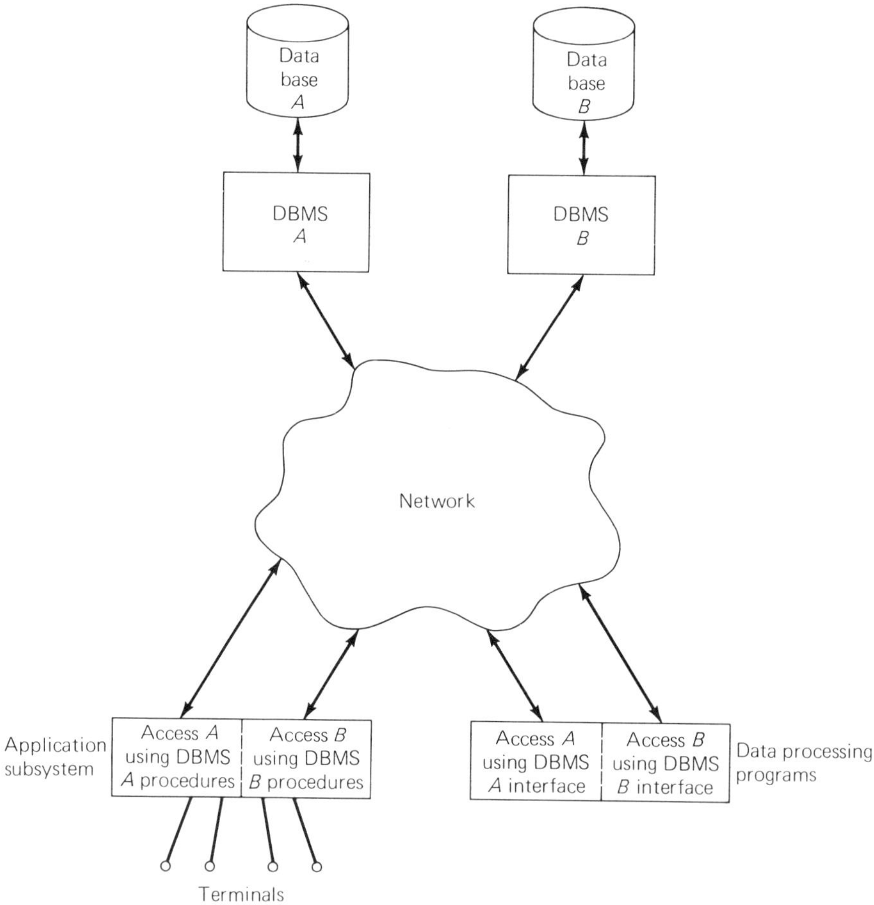

Figure 9.3: One method of access in a multiple DBMS environment is to access each DBMS using its own access procedures

requesting node does the mapping and transmits a message to the responding node in the form of structural information. The data management system in the responding node then performs the file access and returns the desired data to the requesting node.

Multiple Data Base Management Systems

One of the realistic possibilities that has been considered for a distributed data base system environment is the case in which different DBMSs exist in a single computer complex, network, or distributed system. ("Different DBMSs" is intended to mean distinct systems, such as brand A and brand B, rather than multiple versions of the same brand. A distributed data base system in which all DBMSs are the same brand is labeled as *homogeneous.* A distributed data base system in which the DBMSs are of different brands is labeled as *heterogeneous.*)

Access procedures in a multiple DBMS environment can take three forms:

1. Access each DBMS using its own access procedures, as suggested in Figure 9.3.
2. Access all data bases through the access procedures for one of the DBMSs, as suggested in Figure 9.4.
3. Access all data bases through a common query language and interface method, as suggested in Figure 9.5.

Accessing each DBMS using its own access procedures would be cumbersome for a user who needs to reference several data bases simultaneously and would reduce the availability of data—one of the original objectives. One alternative that would be particularly appropriate for a requesting node with the attributes of decentralized organization, distributed network structure, partitioned data base, local directory, and uses one data base system locally would be to access all data base systems using the access procedures for one of the DBMSs—presumably the DBMS used locally. Thus, a translation function would be required for only a small percentage of accesses.

A final alternative is to increase the availability to all data base systems using a common query language and interface method. Using a standardized set of procedures would facilitate file access through a network translation function for each of the DBMSs.

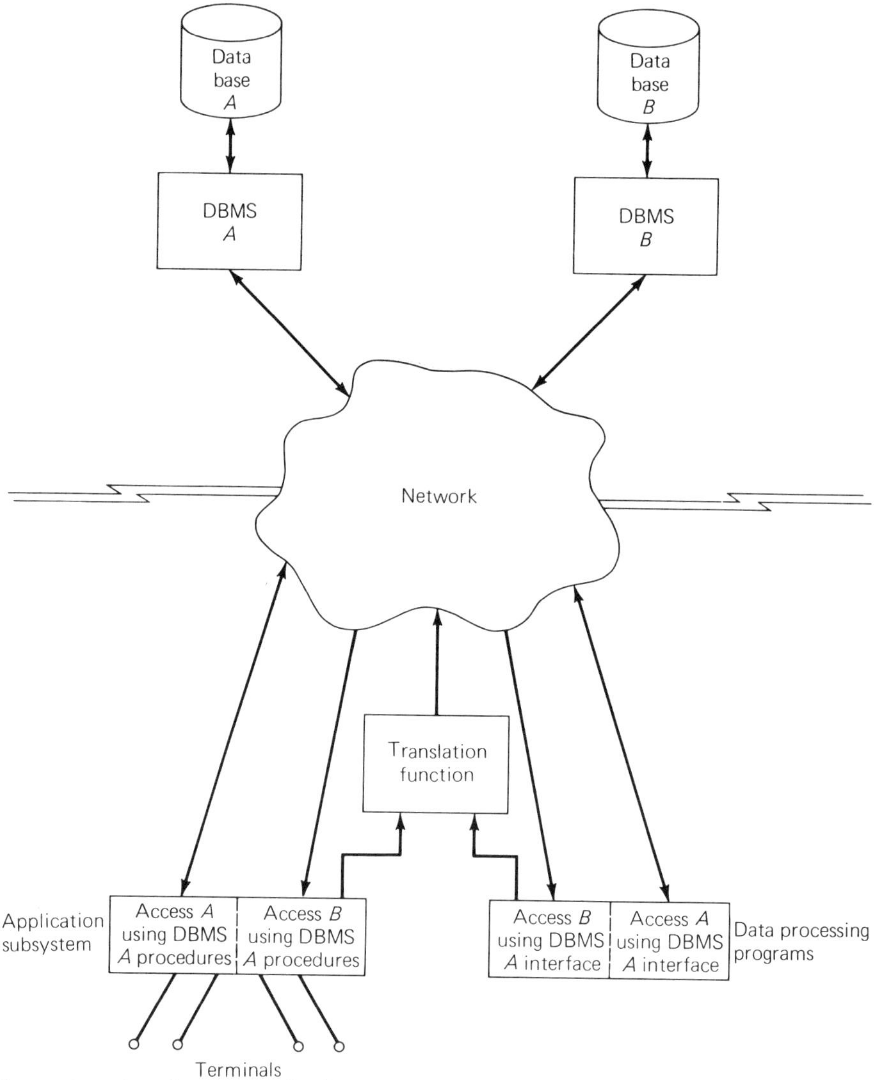

Figure 9.4: Another method of access in a multiple DBMS environment is to access all DBMSs using the access procedures for one of the DBMSs

The existence of multiple DBMSs is a good example of an operating environment in which a switching schema would be employed.

Back-End Computers

One of the options proposed by some system designers is to use a "data base computer," commonly known as a *back-end computer*. The con-

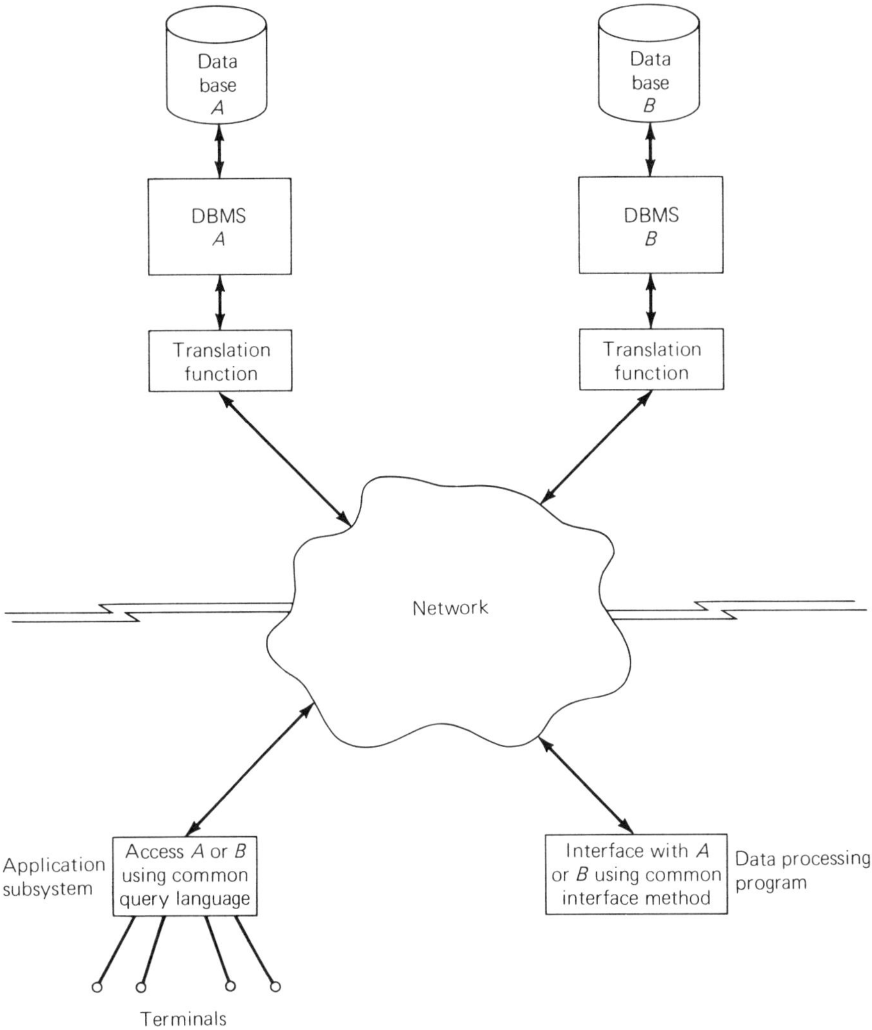

Figure 9.5: A final method of access in a multiple DBMS environment is to access all DBMSs using a common query language and interface method

cept is analogous to the front-end computer used with communications, except that the back-end computer is allocated exclusively to data base functions. Canaday, et al. identify the potential advantages of back-end computers as:

1. Economy through specialization
2. Shared data

3. Data base protection
4. Data base management for new machines[4]

Economy through specialization is an advantage that reduces the load on the host computer. *Shared data* is achieved in a multiple-computer environment because more than one host computer can access the back-end computer. *Data base protection* is achieved because protection measures can be implemented in the back-end computer and a common access path exists. *Data base management for new machines* relates to the fact that through the use of a back-end computer, any computer system can access a data base, and DBMS software need not exist on any or all models of computer. Figure 9.6 depicts two possible uses for a back-end computer in a nondistributed environment.

In a distributed environment, as depicted in Figure 9.7, the use of a back-end computer increases response time, availability, and data integrity for the reasons given above and because all data base messages need not require the services of the host computer.

Split Schema and Subschema

A method that has been proposed for reducing communication costs and increasing the level of load balancing in a distributed system is to split the schema and subschema. Cases wherein the schema and subschema are not

[4]Canaday, R.H.; R.D. Harrison; E.L. Ivie; J.L. Ryder; and L.A. Wehr, "A Back-end Computer for Data Base Management," *Communications of the ACM* 17: 10 (October 1974): 576–577.

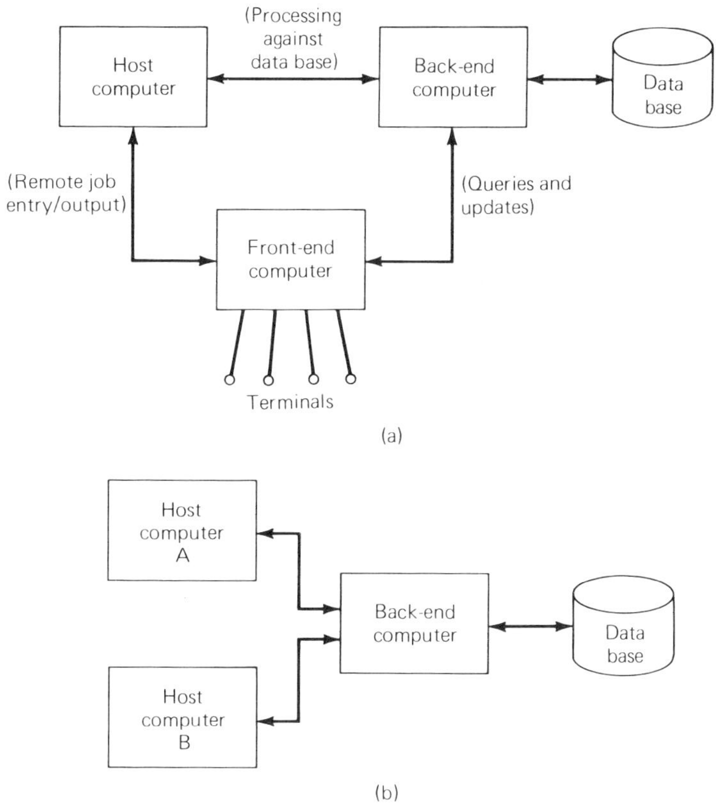

Figure 9.6: Two possible uses for a back-end computer in a nondistributed environment: (a) specialization of function, and (b) access by more than one computer

split are explicitly or implicitly covered in the above discussion. With a split schema or subschema, the schema is stored along with the data base in a responding node, and the subschema is stored in the requesting node. In response to a data request, a record is transmitted to the requesting node from the responding node stored form. Data mapping is then performed at the requesting node by a local DBMS using the subschema.

A Note on Terminology

In order to avoid further confusing the issue by introducing new terminology, the following terms from the literature were used in this chapter:

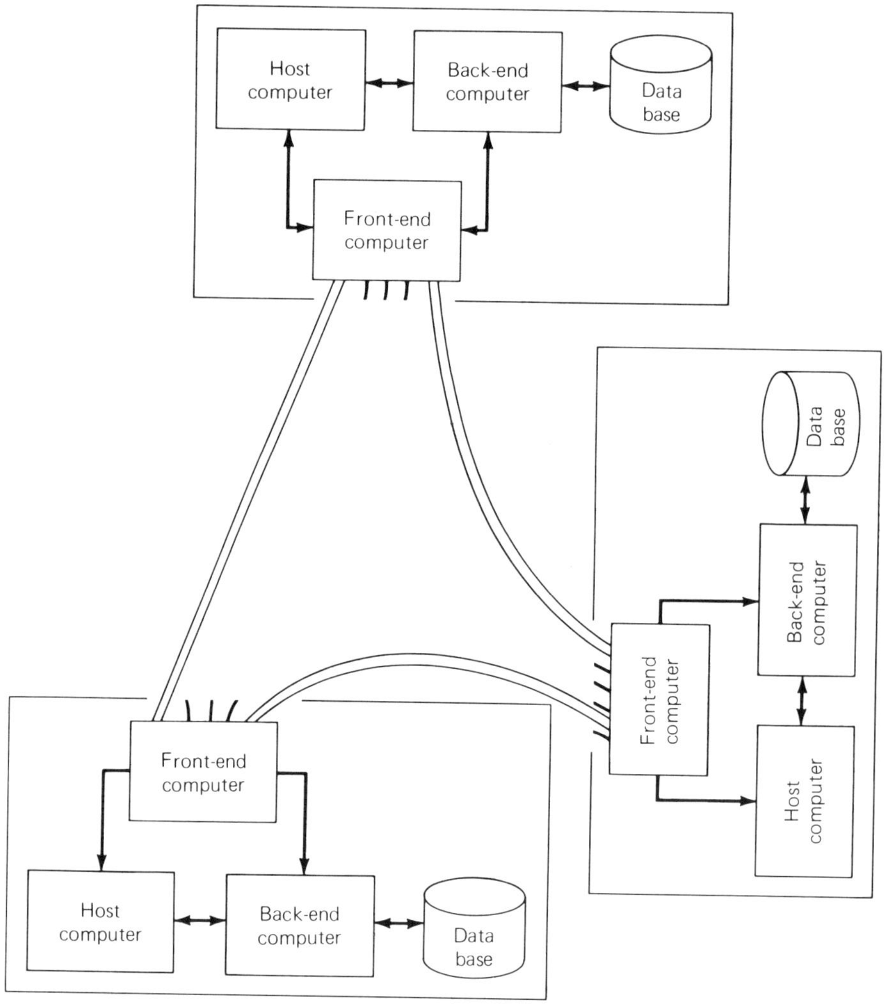

Figure 9.7: The use of a back-end computer in a distribured environment with three different sites

1. For data base architecture

   Centralized, meaning only one copy of the data base in a central computer complex

   Replicated, meaning all or part of the data base is copied in two or more nodes

   Partitioned, meaning that the data resources exist as separate segments with no copies

2. For directory location

   Centralized, meaning a complete directory is located in a central computer complex with possible dispersed subsets for local data bases

   Distributed, meaning a complete copy of the directory resides in two or more nodes

   Local, meaning that a local directory exists for a local data base with no duplication

Obviously, the terminology does not represent the same degree of dividedness. Therefore, the following substitute terminology is proposed for both data base and directory location:

Centralized should imply one copy in a central node

Replicated should imply a complete copy in two or more nodes

Dispersed should imply a complete copy in a central node with possible dispersed subsets

Partitioned should imply separate segments or partitions with no copies

Moreover, it is important to emphasize that the *same* terms should apply to the data base and the directory location.

Summary

A distributed data base system exists when the same groups of data are stored in multiple locations or when data files stored at different locations are interrelated. The basis of a distributed data base system is a data base, defined as a centralized collection of data stored for use in one or more applications. The structural information about a data base is contained in its schema and subschema. The components of a data base system are the schema, the data, and the programs. In a distributed environment, network and communication components are also included.

The architecture of a distributed data base system is designed around two sets of objectives: data base objectives and communications objectives. Data base objectives are availability and integrity. Communications objectives involve the reduction of the number and size of messages and path length between network nodes.

The objectives can be satisfied through the following alternatives:

1. Splitting the data bases
2. Splitting the directories
3. Locating the data base programs

The data base can be centralized, replicated, or partitioned, and the directory location can be centralized, distributed, and local. Distributed data base system characteristics are achieved through various combinations of the above alternatives.

Data base system structure is also important in satisfying objectives and it is dependent upon the relationship between the data base, data base management system (DBMS), and the network. Two options for introducing the network into a system are (1) between the user and the DBMS and (2) between the DBMS and the data base. Another realistic option involves the number and types of DBMSs in a distributed data base system, and special "translation functions" are required for interfacing different DBMSs. Overall network performance can be enhanced through the use of a back-end computer and by splitting the schema and subschema. Lastly, existing terminology is conflicting and confusing and an attempt should be made to clarify its usage.

appendices

A

Effectiveness of Distributed Systems

In earlier days of computers, system effectiveness was an obvious consideration: the hardware was running or it was not running; internal computing speed was well defined; and compile and assemble times were measured in cards per "something." Modern systems, however, very often reside in an operational environment in which either continuous service is required or the mode of operation prevents accurate measurements of throughput or service. Advances in small system organization further complicate the situation. Polymorphic* systems with sophisticated configuration control facilities and distributed systems increase the overall effectiveness but forestall attempts to assign a quantitative value to the increased performance. This apparent concern with effectiveness is well founded. Sophisticated hardware and software facilities are currently available for detecting and recovering from solid, transient, and intermittent errors. In many cases, system functioning can continue but in a degraded mode of operation. The purpose of this appendix is to present general methods which will aid in the synthesis and analysis of both distributed and nondistributed systems. It is expected that the greatest value of this appendix is that it provides a framework for thinking about system effectiveness.

*Informally, a *polymorphic* system is one in which critical components or those that provide significant system resources are duplicated to whatever degree is necessary in order that a desired level of effectiveness is achieved.

Components of System Effectiveness

System effectiveness is a measure of a system's ability to successfully meet an operational demand within a given time when operated under specific conditions. It is a function of some very obvious, but not often discussed, items or components, namely, *mission reliability, operational readiness,* and *functional adequacy.* These items are discussed here to provide background material for the synthesis and analysis techniques which follow later in the appendix.

MISSION RELIABILITY. Mission reliability is a general term coined in the electronics industry by those concerned with reliability. It refers to the probability of a piece of equipment completing a given mission, whether it be a space flight, a bombing pass, or a run on a computer. In the world of computers, the definition is slightly more general. In our case, it refers to the probability of completing a task or session on the computer. Mission reliability is a function of task characteristics, hardware components, network conditions, the load on the system, and the integrity of the software.

OPERATIONAL READINESS. Operational readiness is the probability that the facilities of the system will be available when required. Functionally, it becomes an item of interest once the system or one of its subsystems fails. Moreover, operational readiness relates to maintainability and serviceability in that "down" time is of prime consideration. The capability of partitioning off a maintenance subsystem increases *mission reliability* but also impairs *functional adequacy* in that the system enters a degraded state.

Another important consideration in operational readiness is the installation management policy toward running degraded, i.e., some installations would rather deny than degrade service.

FUNCTIONAL ADEQUACY. Functional adequacy is the relative capacity of the system to perform. Normally, it can be observed as response time or throughput, as the case may be. Within the system, it is related to the amount of system overhead. Another aspect of functional adequacy is the quality of work the user can perform and the ease in doing so. Functional adequacy is affected by the load on the system, parameter adjustments, design and implementation limitations, and the status of the hardware and network configuration. Clearly, it is a measure of a system's ability to perform within limits in the same way the mission reliability measures a system's failure rate.

In actual practice, the effectiveness of a computer system is as dependent upon the job mix, software, and the data base system as it is upon the hardware and network configurations. A comprehensive study of job mixes is unpractical as is an analysis of the various kinds of software. Any software facilities for error recovery and configuration control, however, are dependent upon an appropriate hardware foundation, which can be studied; it is the objective of the remainder of this appendix.

Reliability and Availability

Reliability is the probability that a system will adequately perform its specified function for a specified time under specified conditions. In simple systems, e.g., a computer system consisting of an arithmetic unit, a memory, and an input/output unit, total system failure will result if any of the units fail. In more complex systems, however, the all-or-nothing aspect of failure of a specific unit may result in only degradation of system performance rather than complete failure. In these situations, a system can be in any one of three states: (1) the system will be able to perform all of its functions satisfactorily; (2) one or more unit failures will result in a degradation of performance such that only a fraction of the system's functions can be performed; and (3) failure of more units will cause the system to be totally inoperative. Since reliability is a probability, its value is always between zero and one. Clearly, the reliability of a system is dependent upon two factors: (1) *failure rates* of the components (i.e., mean time to failure); (2) *system organization* (i.e., the manner in which the components are connected, whether it be parallel, serial, or a combination of the two).

Closely related to the concept of reliability is the notion of availability. *Availability (A)* is the probability that a system is available at a time t and is defined as follows:

$$A = \frac{\text{(mean time to failure)}}{\text{(mean time to failure)} + \text{(mean time to repair)}}$$

and *unavailability (U)* is defined accordingly, i.e., $U = 1 - A$.

Availability as defined is a gross time availability or probability of successful operation of a system. It is also of interest to characterize availability in terms of the functions or jobs that the system must perform. Therefore a measure of *functional availability* is required which reflects the probability that input transactions to the system are successfully processed.

Availability is often improved by the use of redundant units. In this regard, switchover time should be considered even though it is not included in the following paragraphs.

Configuration Management

Any system can be broken down into levels of subsystems and finally components. In analyzing a system, subsystems are treated as *units.* In analyzing subsystems, sub-subsystems are treated as units. This process can be continued until the component level is reached. Most systems can be reduced, in a stepwise fashion, to a combination of three basic configurations: series, "M-out-of-N," and parallel.

SERIES. A system which has been organized in *series* is one in which every unit must be functioning for the system to operate. In a system composed of two units, both must be functioning for the system to function. If each unit had an availability of 0.9, then the system would have an availability of 0.81.* Consider also the system pictured as follows:

*A law of probability states that when events are independent (that is, not related), the probability of two events occurring is the product of the individual probabilities of each event occurring. This can be extended to any number of events. The probability of N independent events occurring is merely the product of the probabilities of the N events.

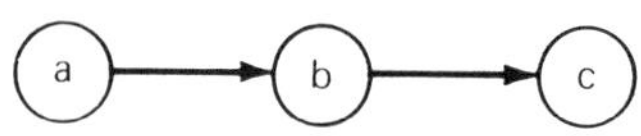

where $A(a) = .9$, $A(b) = .8$, and $A(c) = .7$. The availability of the system composed of units a, b, and c organized serially would be: $A_S = .9 \times .8 \times .7 = .504$. Obvious from these examples is the fact that as the complexity of a series system grows, i.e., as the number of units increases, the availability is decreased.

M-OUT-OF-N. A system configured as an *M-out-of-N* system contains N units of which M must be functioning for the system to operate. Usually, $1 < M < N$. When $M = N$, the M-out-of-N system becomes a series system.

For example, consider the system:

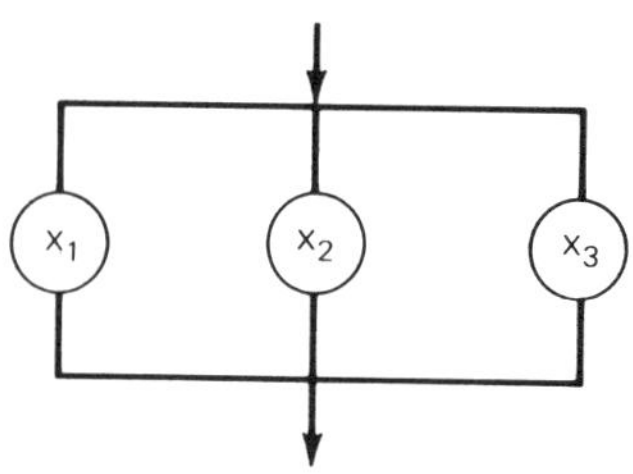

where two of the three units must be functioning for the system to operate. Let $A(x)$ be the availability of unit x and let $U(x)$ be the unavailability of x. The various ways in which the system is operable can now be listed:

1. All three available: $A(x_1) \times A(x_2) \times A(x_3)$
2. x_1 and x_2 available; x_3 unavailable: $A(x_1) \times A(x_2) \times U(x_3)$

3. x_1 and x_3 available; x_2 unavailable: $A(x_1) \times U(x_2) \times A(x_3)$ and
4. x_2 and x_3 available; x_1 unavailable: $U(x_1) \times A(x_2) \times A(x_3)$

It follows the total system availability can be expressed as:

$$A_S = A(x_1) \times A(x_2) \times A(x_3) + A(x_1) \times A(x_2) \times U(x_3) + A(x_1) \times U(x_2) \times A(x_3) + U(x_1) \times A(x_2) \times A(x_3)$$

If $A(x_1) = A(x_2) = A(x_3) = A$, then $A_S = A^3 + 3A^2U$. As an example of what this means, consider the case where $A = 0.9$. Then $A_S = (0.9)^3 + 3\,(0.9)^2(0.1) = 0.972$, with a system unavailability of 0.028. In a series system where two units are required, system availability would be $A_S = 0.9 \times 0.9 = 0.81$ with a system unavailability figure of 0.19. In this case, a 2-out-of-3 configuration such as this reduces the system down time from 19% to 2.8% over a series system.

PARALLEL. A parallel system is a special case of the M-out-of-N system in which $M = 1$. In other words, one unit out of a total of N units need be operable for the system to operate. In a parallel system of two units, only one of the two units is needed for proper system performance. Conversely, both units must fail for the system to fail. Assume that the two units have an availability of 0.90. Then the unavailability of each unit is 0.10. For the system to fail, both units must fail. The probability of this occurring is $0.1 \times 0.1 = 0.01$. Thus, 0.01 is the system unavailability. As previously implied: Availability + Unavailability = 1; therefore, Availability = 1 − Unavailability. Thus, the availability of the parallel system is $1 - 0.01 = 0.99$. By using an extra unit in parallel with the original, the availability of the system can be increased from 90% to 99%. This practice, known as redundancy or duplexing, is generally expensive, but it offers a way to raise the availability of a system far above the level inherent in its individual units or subsystems.

Systems Synthesis

Systems availability is a design consideration. That is, availability is designed into a system and is not something that is tacked on as an afterthought. In synthesizing a system, therefore, the *functional structure* of the system is considered first, or in phase one. Then, *critical subsystems* are identified and redundant units are developed. Later, after a thorough systems analysis, *support units* are included to raise the overall availability values, when required.

The process of system synthesis is demonstrated through the example given in Figure A.1. During phase one, only the functional structure is considered and the system is organized serially. In phase two, subsystem 3 is recognized as a critical subsystem and it is duplexed. Then in phase three, support units are added to increase the overall availability to the required value.

Availability Analysis

Although most availability calculations tend to be intuitive in nature, basic probability theory is required to establish a firm mathematical foundation. The information is presented as two sets of rules; the first governs probability, per se, and the second concerns the assignment of numerical values to events, which will be used when discussing functional availability.

Figure A.1: System synthesis

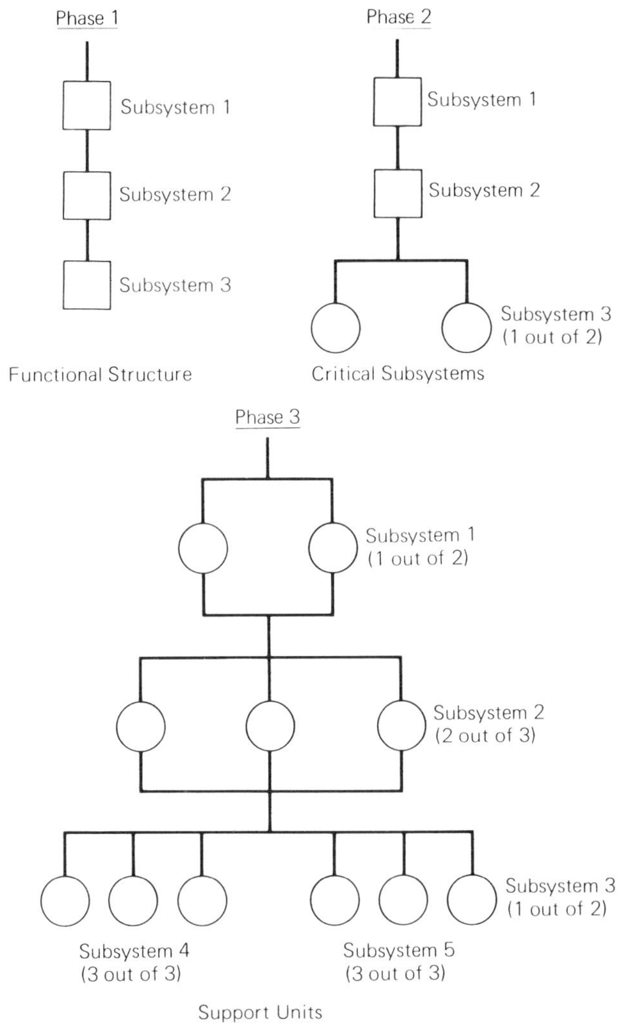

PROBABILITY THEORY. For the needs of this appendix, *probability* theory is summarized by the following rules:

1. A probability is a number between 0 and 1 assigned to an event.
2. The sum of the probabilities assigned to a set of mutually exclusive events must be 1. (Two events are mutually exclusive if it is impossible for both to take place.)
3. The probability that one or the other of two mutually exclusive events will take place is the sum of their probabilities.

4. The probability that both of two independent events will take place is the product of their separate probabilities. (Two events are independent if the outcome of the first does not affect the probability that the second will occur.)
5. The probability that both of two dependent events will occur is the probability of the first multiplied by the probability which the second will have if the first has already occurred.

The second area of interest concerns the functional value of a system and involves the capability of the system, from an availability point of view, to handle a predetermined work load. The process involves the following steps:

1. Assigning a definite numerical *value* to every consequence.
2. Assigning a definite numerical *weight* (i.e., probability) to every event.
3. Evaluating the system by taking a *weighted average* of all the different values which might result from each consequence.

Each of the values which have been assigned in step 1 above is the value which some particular consequence will have on condition that that particular event occurs; therefore, these values are called *conditional values.* After probabilities are assigned to events in step 2, step 3 consists of obtaining a single functional value by taking a weighted average of all the various conditional values, each conditional value being weighted by the probability that the respective consequence will indeed occur. The standard name for this weighted average is the *expected value.*

Table A.1: Configurations of three units

TYPE	UNITS REQUIRED	FUNCTIONAL REQUIREMENTS	AVAILABILITY EQUATION
Series	All three	———	$A_S = A^3$
Parallel	One of three	Three operable Two operable (3 ways) One operable (3 ways)	$A_S = A^3 + 3A^2U + 3AU^2$ or $A_S = A^3 - 3A^2 + 3A$
M-out-of-N	Two of three	Three operable Two operable	$A_S = A^3 + 3A^2U$ or $A_S = 3A^2 - 2A^3$

THE GENERAL AVAILABILITY EQUATION. As illustration of the various availabilities associated with different configurations, the different ways in which three units can be connected are given in Table A.1, where A and U represent availability and unavailability, respectively.

It was mentioned earlier that the series configuration and the parallel configuration were special cases of the M-out-of-N system. Considering the equations in Table A.1, it is also seen that a pattern appears to exist among the equations for the various types. As it turns out, the availability equations for the three methods of configuration can be represented by one general-purpose multiple-component availability equation, when the unit availabilities are the same. It is presented without proof as follows

$$A_S = A^n + \sum_{k=1}^{n-m} \frac{n!}{k!\,(n-k)!} A^{n-k}(1-A)^k$$

where n is the number of identical units in the subsystem and m is the number of them that are required for the subsystem to function. Although its use from a total systems viewpoint is limited, it eliminates the necessity of undertaking a probabilistic analysis for each subsystem being studied.

SYSTEM ANALYSIS. When analyzing the availability of a system, two conditions are usually considered: (1) the availability limits required by the system; and (2) the availability specifications for each of the component units. The basic problem, of course, is one of determining when a given configuration satisfies requirements. The *availability graph* is useful for this purpose and for descriptive purposes, as well. It is introduced through the next example.

Consider a function to be performed that requires one unit. Two design choices are possible: a single unit can be employed, or if greater availability is desired, a second unit can be added in parallel:

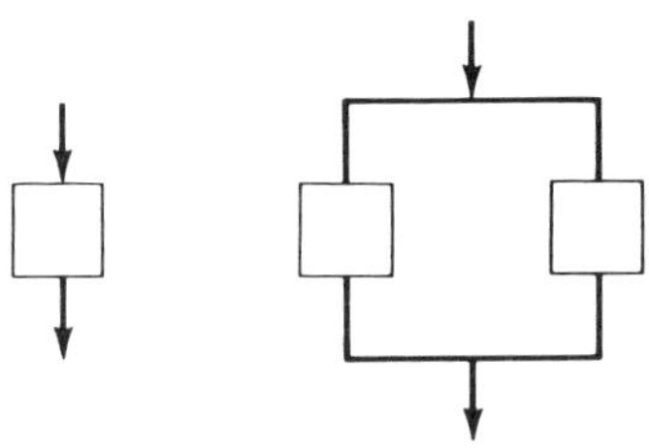

System X $A_S = A$ System Y $A_S = 2A - A^2$

Also assume that unit availability is 0.75 and the minimum system availability requirement is 0.85. Obviously, System X does not meet requirements but as shown in the availability graph of Figure A.2, System Y does. Closely related to the availability graph is the *unavailability graph,* which is computed from availability data by the relation $U = 1 - A$. An unavailability graph for the preceding examples is also given in Figure A.2.

As a second example, consider an application that requires two identical units. Two units could be used or, to increase availability, a third unit could be added as a spare:

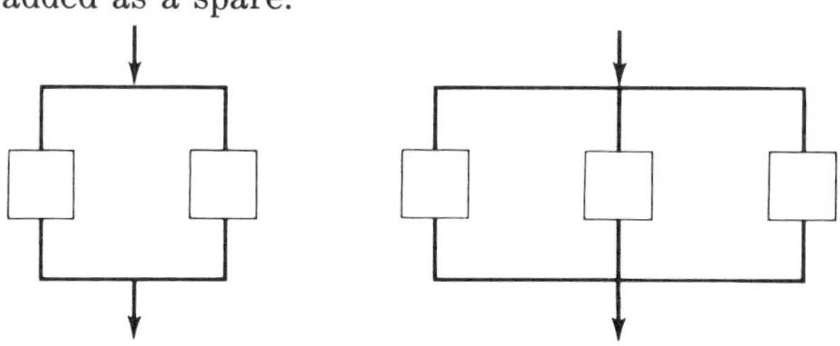

System Z System W

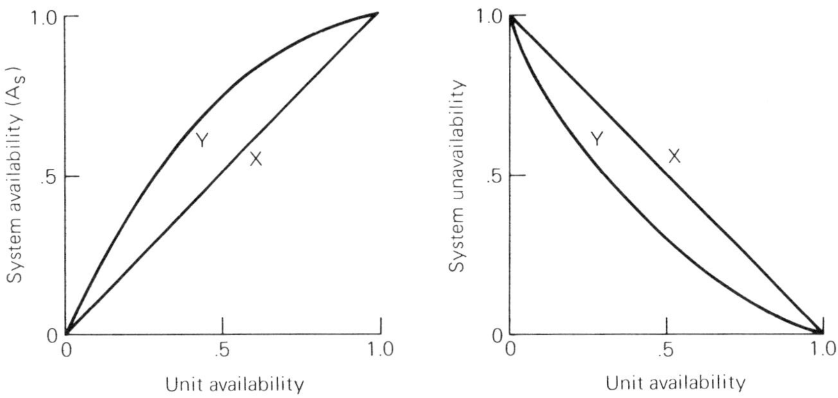

Figure A.2: Availability and unavailability graphs

Figure A.3:
Availability graph for a 2-out-of-2 vs. a 2-out-of-e system

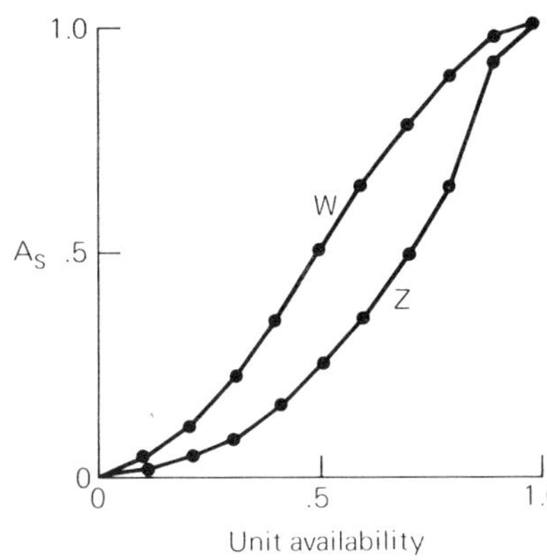

Clearly, System Z is a series system since both units must be functioning for the system to operate. System W, however, is a M-out-of-N system since only 2 of the 3 units need be operational. The availability of System Z is A^2, while the availability of System W is: $A_S = A^3 + 3A^2U = 3A^2 - 2A^3$. Figure A.3 contains an availability graph for this system and demonstrates the significant increase in system availability which can be achieved by adding a spare unit.

It is evident from the above examples that analysis techniques are intuitive. The availability equation and the availability graph provide a means of summarizing and of presenting availability data, respectively. Most systems, however, are more complex than these examples and do not lend themselves to easy analysis. The key steps in systems analysis, therefore, are those which relate to the operational environment, i.e., the nature of the installations work load, and those which involve the interpretation of the availability data in light of defined installation objectives. The operational environment is considered in the next section.

Functional Availability

One of the major factors in the operational environment is whether or not the system is in the proper state to handle individual requests for service, at a given point in time. As the work load fluctuates with time, the extent to which the system can process these requests is known as functional availability. More formally, *functional availability* is the probability that a request for service can successfully be processed according to specified installation guidelines. Functional availability is affected by three factors:

1. The probability that the system is in a particular internal state (for example, all units working, one unit down, etc.)
2. The percentage of input requests that occur during peak and nonpeak periods of a day
3. The percentage of requests that can be handled in each internal state

The concept is further introduced through an example. Consider, for example, the following configuration which might represent some sort of data processing system:

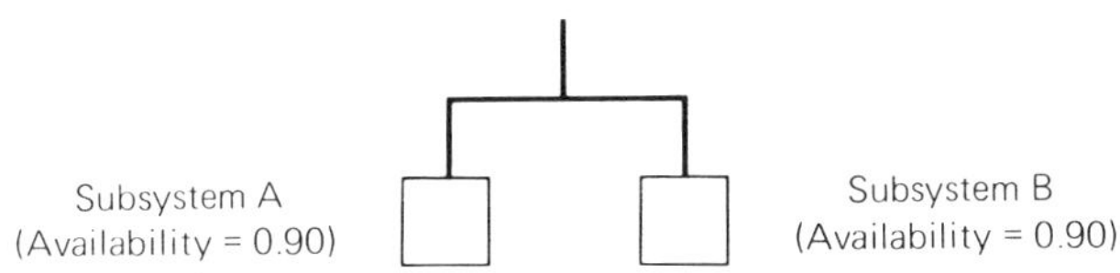

The system operating time is divided into two periods: peak periods and nonpeak periods. During nonpeak periods, either subsystem can process all requests for service. Nonpeak periods handle 40% of the total work load. During peak periods, both subsystems must be functioning in order that all requests are successfully processed. When one unit is down, however, 80% of the requests can be processed by the other subsystem. This represents *partial capability* of 80%. Peak periods account for 60% of the total work load. Before total system or overall functional availability can be calculated, it is first necessary to calculate the following items: (1) the probabilities that one and two units are available; and (2) the percentages of input requests that are successfully processed during peak and nonpeak periods using the probabilities obtained in (1).

The probability that *at least* one unit is available is

$$A_S = A^2 + \sum_{k=1}^{1} \frac{2!}{k!\,(2 - k!)} A^{2-k} (1 - A)^k = 2A - A^2$$

while the probability that two units are available is A^2. It follows that the probability that *exactly* one unit is available is $(2A - A^2) - A^2 = 2A - 2A^2$.

The percentages which are required for item (2) can now be computed from the following general equation:

$$A_F = (\text{Capability when 1 unit is up}) \times (\text{Probability of only 1 unit up}) + (\text{Capability when 2 units are up}) \times (\text{Probability of 2 units up})$$

Recalling that during nonpeak periods the system has 100% capability when either one or two units are up, then functional availability for this time period is:*

$$A_F(\text{nonpeak}) = (1.0) \times (0.18) + (1.0) \times (0.81) = 0.99$$

The calculations are similar during peak hours where the system has 100% capability with two units and an 80% partial capability with exactly one unit. Functional availability for this period is:

$$A_F(\text{peak}) = (0.8)(0.18) + (1.0)(0.81) = 0.954$$

Overall functional availability combines the functional availabilities for each of the two time periods with 60% of the requests being processed during peak hours and 40% during nonpeak hours. The two individual functional availabilities are combined in the following equation to compute the *overall functional availability:*

$$\begin{aligned} A_F(\text{overall}) &= 0.60 \times A_F(\text{peak}) + 0.40 \times A_F(\text{nonpeak}) \\ &= 0.60 \times 0.954 + 0.40 \times 0.99 \\ &= 0.968 \end{aligned}$$

*Using an Availability of 0.90, the probability of two units being up is A^2 or 0.81 and the probability of exactly one unit being up is $2A - 2A^2$ or 0.18.

On the average, then almost 97% of the requests for service can be satisfied by this system. Of equal importance are the 3% that cannot be satisfied. If the situation could not be handled by backup procedures, then a system analysis followed by a partial redesign would be necessary.

Summary

In modern systems, methods are available for increasing overall system effectiveness but it is frequently difficult to assign a quantitative value to the increased performance. System effectiveness is a measure of a system's ability to successfully meet an operational demand within a given time when operated under specified conditions. It is a function of mission reliability, operational readiness, and functional adequacy. Reliability is the probability that a system will adequately perform its specified function for a specified time under specified conditions. Availability is a gross time probability of successful operation of a system.

The objective of reliability and availability analysis is configuration management. Three basic configurations are: series, M-out-of-N, and parallel. Systems are analyzed through availability analysis and the use of availability graphs. An operational method of analysis involves functional availability, which is the probability that a service request can be successfully processed by a system.

The purpose of this appendix is to exemplify varied techniques for determining system effectiveness. The methods are general in nature and can be used for systems that are too complex for or not described well enough for mathematical analysis.

B

Guide to Abbreviations and Acronyms in Data Communications

A/D	Analog/digital
ACF	Advanced communications function
ACK	Acknowledgement, positive
ACKO, ACKl	Affirmative acknowledgement
ACU	Automatic calling unit
ADCCP	Advanced Data Communications Control Procedure (American National Standard)
AM	Amplitude modulation
ANSI	American National Standards Institute
ARPA	Advanced Research Project Agency (Department of Defense)
Arpanet	ARPA network (Department of Defense)
ARQ	Automatic request for repetition
ASCII	American Standard Code for Information Interchange
ASR	Automatic send/receive
Autodin	Automatic digital network (Department of Defense)
AVD	Alternate voice/data
Baudot	Teleprinter code (5 level)
BC	Block check
BCC	Block check character
BCD	Binary coded decimal
BDLC	Burroughs Data Link Control (Burroughs Corporation)
BISYNC	Binary Synchronous Communications
BIT	Binary digit
BIU	Basic Information Unit
BLU	Basic Link Unit
BPS	Bits per second
BSC	Binary Synchronous Communications

BTAM	Basic Telecommunications Access Method
BTU	Basic Transmission Unit
CBX	Computerized private branch exchange
CCB	Common Carrier Bureau
CCF	Communications control field
CCIS	Common channel interoffice system (AT&T)
CCITT	Comite Consultatif Internationale de Telegraphie et Telephonie
CCT	Coupler cut through
CCU	Communications control unit
CDC	Call directing code
CDCCP	Control Data communications control procedure (Control Data Corporation)
CDF	Communications-data field
CMDR	Command reject
Coax	Coaxial cable
Comsat	Communications Satellite Corporation
CP	Connection point
CPODA	Contention priority-oriented demand assignment (protocol)
CPU	Central processing unit
CR	Carriage return
CRC	Cyclic redundancy check
CRT	Cathode ray tube
CTS	Communications Technology Satellite or clear to send
Cybernet	Control Data Corporation network
DA	Data available
DAA	Data access arrangement
DAF	Destination address field

DAL	Data access line
DAP	Data access protocol
Dataset	Synonym for modem (see modem)
DCE	Data communication equipment
DCS	Distributed computing system
DDCMP	Digital Data Communications Message Protocol
DDD	Direct distance dialing
DDP	Distributed data processing
DDS	Data-Phone Digital Service
Decnet	Digital Equipment Corporation network
DES	Data encryption standard
DFC	Data flow control
DISC	Disconnect
DLC	Data link control
DLCF	Data link control field
DLE	Data link escape
DMA	Direct memory address
DNA	Digital network architecture (Digital Equipment Corporation)
Domsat	Domestic satellite service
DOS	Disk operating system
DSC	Direct satellite communications
DSDS	Dataphone switched digital service (AT&T)
DSE	Distributed system environment
DSU	Data service unit
DTE	Data terminal equipment
EBCDIC	Extended Binary Coded Decimal Interchange Code
EFT	Electronic funds transfer
EIA	Electronic Industries Association

EOA	End of address
EOM	End of message
EOT	End of text or end of transmission
ESS	Electronic switching system
ENQ	Enquiry
ETB	End of text block
ETX	End of text
FAX	Facsimile
FCC	Federal Communications Commission
FCS	Frame check sequence
FDM	Frequency division multiplexing
FDX	Full-duplex transmission
FEC	Forward error correction
FED-STD	Federal standard
-1001	High-speed synchronous signaling rates between data terminal equipment and data circuit-terminating equipment
-1003	Bit-oriented data link control procedures
-1005	2.4 kbit/s modems
-1010	ASCII bit sequencing for serial-by-bit transmission
-1011	Character structure for serial-by-bit ASCII transmission
-1012	Character structure for parallel-by-bit ASCII transmission
-1013	Data terminal equipment to data circuit-terminating equipment synchronous signaling rates using 4 Hz circuits
-1020	Electrical characteristics of unbalanced voltage digital interface circuits
-1030	Electrical

	characteristics of balanced voltage digital interface circuits
FID	Format identification
FIFO	First in, first out
FIGS	Figures shift (teleprinters)
FIPS	Federal Information Processing Standards
FM	Frequency modulation or function management
FOC	Fiber optics communications
FSK	Frequency shift keying
FX	Foreign exchange
HDLC	High level Data Link Control (International Standards Organization)
HDX	Half-duplex transmission
IMP	Interface message processor
Infonet	Computer Science Corporation network
Intelsat	International satellite service
IS	International standard
IS-646-1973	Bit-coded character set for information processing interchange
IS 1155-1973	Information processing—use of longitudinal parity to detect errors in information messages (included in V.4 and X.4)
IS 1177-1973	Information processing—character structure for start/stop and synchronous transmission (included in V.4 and X.4)
IS 1745-1975	Information processing—basic mode control

	procedures for data communications systems
IS 2110-1972	Data communication —data terminal and data communication equipment—interchange circuits. Assignment of connector pin numbers (being revised—DIS 2110 is being balloted)
IS 2111-1972	Data communication —basic mode control procedures—code independent information transfer
IS 2593-1973	Connector pin allocations for use with high-speed data terminal equipment
IS 2628-1973	Basic mode control procedures—complements
IS 2629-1973	Basic mode control procedures—conversational information message transfer
IS 3309-1976	Data communications —high-level data link control procedures—frame structure
IS 4335-1977	Data communications —high-level data link control procedures—elements of procedures (independent numbering)
ISO	International Standards Organization
ITDM	Intelligent time-division multiplexer
ITS	Invitation to send
ITU	International Telecommunications Union
KAK	Key-auto-key
KAU	Keystation adapter unit

KDS	Keyboard display station
KSR	Keyboard send/receive
LDM	Limited-distance modem
LIFO	Last in, first out
LIM	Line interface module
LIU	Line interface unit
LO	Line occupancy
LRC	Longitudinal redundancy checking
LSD	Line-sharing device or line signal detector
LTRS	Letters shift (teletypewriters)
LU	Logical unit
Merit	Michigan network among three largest universities
MIU	Multistation interface unit
MNCS	Multipoint network-control system
MODEM	Modulator-Demodulator
MPCC	Multiprotocol communications controller
MPL	Multischedule private line
MTBF	Mean time between failures
MTTR	Mean time to repair
NAK	Negative acknowledgement
NAM	Network access method (Control Data Corporation)
NAU	Network accessable unit
NBS	National Bureau of Standards
NC	Network control
NCP	Network control program (IBM)
NCR-DNA	NCR Corporation-distributed network architecture
NDM	Normal disconnected mode

NRM	Normal response mode
NRZ	Non-return to zero (waveform)
NRZI	Non-return to zero inverted
NS	Network services
NSA	Nonsequenced acknowledgement
NSI	Nonsequenced information frame
NSP	Network services protocol (Digital Equipment Corp.) and nonsequenced poll
OAF	Origin address field
Octopus	Control Data Corporation network
OS	Operating system
PABX	Private automatic branch exchange
PAD	Packet assembler/ disassembler
PAM	Pulse amplitude modulation
PBX	Private branch exchange
PC	Path control
PCM	Pulse code modulation
P/F	Poll/Final bit
PIU	Path information unit
PM	Phase modulation
PMS	Public message service (WU)
PMX	Packet multiplexer
PS	Presentation services
PSC	Public Service Commission
PSE	Packet-switching exchange
PTT	Post, Telephone, and Telegraph Authority
PU	Physical unit
PUC	Public Utilities Commission
QTAM	Queued telecommunications access method
RAS	Reliability, availability, and serviceability

RCD	Receiver-carrier detector
RDC	Remote data concentrator
REJ	Reject
RH	Request-response header
RNR	Receive not ready
ROL	Request online status
RQI	Request initialization
RR	Receive ready
RS	Recommended standard (EIA)
RS-232-C	Interface between data terminal equipment and data communication equipment employing serial binary data interchange (August 1969)
RS-269-B	Synchronous signaling rates for data transmission (January 1976; identical to ANSI X3. 1-1976)
RS-334	Signal quality at interface between data processing terminal equipment and synchronous data communication equipment for serial data transmission (also adopted as ANSI X3.24-1967; new revision being balloted)
RS-357	Interface between facsimile terminal equipment and voice frequency data communication terminal equipment (June 1968)
RS-363	Standard for specifying signal quality for transmitting and receiving data processing terminal equipment using serial data transmission at the interface with non-synchronous data communication

equipment (May 1969)

RS-366 — Interface between data terminal equipment and automatic calling equipment for data communication (August 1969)

RS-404 — Standard for start/stop signal quality between data terminal equipment and non-synchronous data communication equipment (March 1973)

RS-410 — Standard for electrical characteristics of Class A closure interchange circuits (April 1974)

RS-422 — Electrical characteristics of balanced voltage digital interface circuits (April 1975)

RS-423 — Electrical characteristics of unbalanced voltage digital interface circuits (April 1975)

RTS — Request to send

RU — Request-Response Unit

RVI — Reverse interrupt

SABRE — Semi-Automatic Business Research Environment

SAGE — Semi-Automatic Ground Environment

SC — Session control

SCC — Satellite communications controller or specialized common carrier

SDLC — Synchronous Data Link Control (IBM)

SIM — Set initialization mode

SIMP — Satellite information message protocol

SMRT	Single message rate timing
SNA	Systems Network Architecture (IBM)
SNAP	Standard network access protocol
SNR	Signal-to-noise ratio
SNRM	Set normal response mode
SOH	Start of header
SOM	Start of message
SP	Space character
SQD	Signal quality detector
SSCP	System Services Control Point
STD	Subscriber trunk dialing
STR	Synchronous transmit/receive (4 level code, IBM)
STX	Start of text
SU	Signaling unit
SVD	Simultaneous voice/data
Swift	Society for Worldwide Interbank Financial Telecommunications (banking network)
SYN	Synchronous idle
TAC	Telenet access controller (Telenet Corporation)
TC	Terminal controller or transmission control
TCAM	Telecommunications access method
TCU	Transmission control unit
TDM	Time-division multiplexer
Telex	Teleprinter exchange service (WU)
TEST	Test
TH	Transmission header
TIMS	Transmission impairment measuring set (Hewlett-Packard)
TIP	Terminal interface package
TMS	Telecommunications message switcher

TMU	Transmission message unit
TNS	Transaction network service (AT&T)
TP	Teleprocessing
TTD	Temporary text delay
TTY	Teletypewriter
TWX	Teletypewriter Exchange Service
Tymnet	Timeshare Inc. network
UART	Universal asynchronous receiver/transmitter
UDLC	Universal Data Link Control (Sperry UNIVAC)
USASCII	United States of America Standard Code for Information Interchange
USITA	United States Independent Telephone
V.	CCITT code designation
V.1	Equivalence between notation symbols and the significant conditions of a two-condition code
V.2	Power levels for data transmission over telephone lines
V.3	International alphabet No. 5
V.4	General structure of signals of international alphabet No. 5 code for data transmission over public telephone network
V.10 (X.26)	Electrical characteristics for unbalanced double-current interchange circuits for general use with integrated circuit equipment in the field of data communications (and provisional

	amendments, May 1977)
V.11 (X.27)	Electrical characteristics for balanced double-current interchange circuits for general use with integrated circuit equipment in the field of data communications (and provisional amendments, May 1977)
V.15	Use of acoustic coupling for data transmission
V.19	Modems for parallel data transmission using telephone signaling frequencies
V.20	Parallel data transmission modems standardized for universal use in the general switched telephone network
V.21	200-bit/s modem standardized for use in the general switched telephone network
V.22	Standardization of data signaling rates for synchronous data transmission in the general switched telephone network
V.22bis	Standardization of data signaling rates for synchronous data transmission on leased telephone-type circuits
V.23	600/1.2K bit/s modem standardized for use in the general switched telephone network
V.24	List of definitions for interchange circuits between data terminal equipment and data circuit terminating

	equipment (and provisional amendments, May 1977)		standardized for use on the one leased circuits
		V.27ter	4.8K/2.4K bit/s modem standardized for use in the general switched telephone network
V.25	Automatic calling and/or answering equipment on the general switched telephone network, including disabling of echo suppressors on manually established calls	V.28	Electrical characteristics for unbalanced double-current interchange circuits
V.26	2.4K/1.2K bit/s modem standardized for use on four-wire leased circuits	V.29	9.6 kbit/s modem for use on leased circuits
V.26bis	2.4K/1.2K bit/s modem standardized for use in the general switched telephone network	V.31	Electrical characteristics for single-current interchange circuits controlled by contact closure
V.27	4.8 kbit/s modem standardized for use on leased circuits	V.35	Data transmission at 48 kbit/s using 60-to-108 kHz group-bit/s circuits
V.27bis	4.8 kbit/s modem with automatic equalizer	V.36	Modems for synchronous data transmission using

	60-to-108 kHz group-bit/s circuits
V.41	Code independent control system
V.54	Loop test devices for modems (and provisional amendments, May 1977)
VAC	Value added carrier
VAN	Value added network
VAS	Value added service
VRC	Vertical redundancy checking
VTAM	Virtual telecommunications access method (IBM)
WACK	Wait before transmitting positive acknowledgement
WATS	Wide area telephone service
X.	CCITT recommendation designation
X.1	International user classes of service in public data networks
X.2	International user facilities in public data networks
X.3	Packet assembly/disassembly facility (PAD) in a public data network
X.4	General structure of signals of international alphabet No. 5 code for data transmission over public data networks
X.20	Interface between data terminal equipment and data circuit-terminating equipment for start/stop transmission services on public data networks
X.20bis (V.21)	Compatible interface between data terminal equipment

	and data circuit-terminating equipment for start/stop transmission services on public data networks
X.21	General purpose interface between data terminal equipment and data circuit-terminating equipment for synchronous operation on public data networks
X.21bis	Use on public data networks of data terminal equipment which is designed for interfacing to synchronous V-series modems
X.24	List of definitions of interchange circuits between data terminal equipment and data circuit-terminating equipment on public data networks
X.25	Interface between data terminal equipment and data circuit-terminating equipment for terminals operating in the packet mode on public data networks (and provisional amendment, April 1977)
X.26	Electrical characteristics for unbalanced double-current interchange circuits for general use with integrated circuit equipment in the field of data communications (identical to V.10)
X.27	Electrical characteristics for

balanced double-current interchange circuits for general use with integrated circuit equipment in the field of data communications (identical to V.11)

V.28 DTE/DCE interface for start/stop mode data terminal equipment accessing the packet assembly/ disassembly facility (PAD) on a public network situated in the same country

X.29 Procedures for exchange of control information and user data between a packet-mode DTE and a packet assembly/ disassembly facility (PAD)

X.30 Standardization of basic model page-printing machine in accordance with international alphabet No. 5

X.31 Characteristics, from the transmission point of view, at the interchange point between data terminal equipment and data circuit-terminating equipment in a 200 bit/s start/stop data terminal

X.32 Answer-back units for 200 bit/s start/stop machines in accordance with international alphabet No. 5

X.33 Standardization of an international text for the measurement of the margin of

	start/stop machines in accordance with international alphabet No. 5
X.92	Hypothetical reference connections for public synchronous data networks
X.95	Network parameters in public data networks
X.96	Call progress signals in public data networks
X3.1-1976	Synchronous signaling rates for data transmission
X3.15-1976	Bit sequencing of the American national standard code for information interchange in serial-by-bit transmission
X3.16-1976	Character structure and character parity sense for serial-by-bit data communication in the American national standard code for information interchange
X3.25-1976	Character structure and character parity sense for parallel-by-bit communication in the American national standard code for information interchange
X3.28-1976	Procedures for the use of communication control characters of American national standard code for information interchange in specified data communications links
X3.36-1977	Synchronous high-speed data signaling rates between data terminal equipment and data

	communication equipment
X3.44-1977	Determination of the performance of data communication systems
X3.57-1977	Message heading formats for information interchange using ASCII for data communication system control
XID	Exchange Station Identification

C

Guide to Data Communications Buzzwords

ACK. (affirmative acknowledgement). Used in block transmission, indicates that the previous transmission block was accepted by the receiver and that it is ready to accept the next block of the transmission.

ASCII. 8 level code (7 bits + parity) from American Standard Code for Information Interchange.

ALPHAMERIC. (Same meaning as "alphanumeric".). A generic term for alphabetic letters, numerical digits, and special characters which are machine-processable. Used to describe a character set that contains both letters and digits and, usually, other characters such as punctuation marks and symbols.

ASYNCHRONOUS TRANSMISSION. Transmission in which each information character is individually synchronized, usually by the use of start and stop elements.

ATTENUATION. A decrease in power usually measured in decibels.

AUTOMATIC CALLING UNIT. A device which permits a business machine to dial calls automatically.

BPS. (bits per second) In serial transmission, the instantaneous bit speed within one character, as transmitted by a machine or channel.

BTAM. (basic telecommunications access method) Used to control the transfer of data between main storage and local or remote terminals. BTAM provides the applications program with macro instructions for using the capabilities of the

Reprinted by permission of Racal-Milgo, Inc. from *Sherry's Guide to Data Communications Buzzwords.*

devices supported. BTAM supports binary synchronous (bi-sync) as well as start/stop communication.

BATCH PROCESSING. A system of accumulation and grouping a number of similar input items for processing at one time.

BANDWIDTH. The difference in cycles per second, or hertz, between the high and low frequencies of a band.

BAUD. A unit of signaling speed equal to the number of shortest signal events per second.

BAUDOT CODE. A 5-bit telegraphy code utilizing start and stop elements.

BINARY SYNCHRONOUS COMMUNICATIONS. A line control procedure for communicating. It can be expressed in several data codes: 8-bit EBCDIC, 7-bit USASCII, or 6-bit transcode. The only requirements are that the code should include the required line control characters and that these characters should be used according to specified rules.

BIT. The smallest unit of information in a binary system of notation.

BUFFER. A storage device that compensates for a difference in rate of flow of data, or time of occurrence of events, when transmitting data from one devicc to another.

CCITT. The Consultive Committee International Telegraph and Telephone is an advisory committee established under the United Nations within the International Telecommunications Union (ITU) to recommend worldwide standards.

CICS. (customer information control system) CICS provides an interface between the operating system access methods and applications programs to allow remote or local display terminal interaction with the data base in the central processor. Different versions include Time Management facilities and support for bi-sync, dial-up, PL 1 support and expanded data base control items such as file browsing, dynamic file open and close.

CPU. (central processing unit) A unit of a computer that includes the circuits controlling the interpretation and execution of instructions. Synonymous with main frame.

CARRIER SYSTEM. A method of deriving two or more simultaneous continuous channels over a medium connecting two points by assigning separate portions of the bandwidth to the individual channels.

CRT. (cathode ray tube) An electronic vacuum tube, such as a television picture tube, that can be used to display images.

CENTRAL OFFICE. The place where communications common carriers terminate customer lines and locate equipment which connects those lines.

CHANNEL. A path for electrical transmission. Also called circuit, facility, line, link or path.

CHARACTER. The actual or coded representation of a digit, letter, or special symbol.

CIRCUIT. A communications path between two points.

CLOCK. A source of precisely spaced timing pulses.

COAXIAL CABLE. A cable consisting of an outer conductor concentric to an inner conductor, separated from each other by insulating material.

CODE. A system of symbols and rules for use in representing information.

COMMON CARRIER. A government-regulated company which furnishes public telecommunications facilities such as a telephone or telegraph company.

COMPANDOR. A device placed on a telephone circuit that compresses and expands the speech volume for an improvement in signal to noise ratio.

CONDITIONING. The addition of equipment to a leased voice-grade channel to provide minimum values of line characteristics required for data transmission.

CONTENTION. A method of line control in which the terminals request to transmit. If the channel in question is free, transmission goes ahead. If not, the terminal will have to wait until it becomes free. The queue of contention requests may be built up by the computer.

CONTROL STATION. The station (usually a CPU) in a multipoint data communications system that controls network traffic by means of polling and selection.

CROSS TALK. An unwanted signal from one transmission circuit detected on another circuit.

CURSOR. A character-position marker which may be moved manually, as used in the 40+ CRT display.

DBM. Decibel referenced to one milliwatt. Employed in communication work as a measure of power. Zero dBm equals 1 milliwatt.

DATA. A representation of facts, concepts, or instructions in a formalized manner suitable for communication, interpretation, or processing by human beings or automatic means; any representation, such as characters, to which meaning might be assigned.

DATA-ACQUISITION. The process of identifying, isolating, and gathering source data to be centrally processed in a usable form.

DATA COLLECTION. The act of bringing data from one or more points to a central point.

DATA COMMUNICATION. The movement of information by an electrical transmission system.

DATA-PHONE. TM A trademark of the A.T.&T. Company to identify the data sets manufactured and supplied by the Bell System for transmitting data over the telephone network. It is also a Bell System service mark to identify the transmission of data over the telephone network (Data-Phone Service).

DDS. Data-Phone Digital ServiceTM is a trademark of the A.T.&T. Company to identify a private line, interstate service for digital data communications.

DATA PROCESSING. (same as "information processing") The execution of a systematic sequence of operations performed upon data.

DATA PROCESSING SYSTEM. A network of machine components capable of accepting information, processing it according to a plan and producing the desired results.

DATA SET. A device which performs modulation/demodulation and control functions to provide compatibility between business machines and communication lines for transmission over these lines.

DATA SOURCE. The equipment which supplies data signals to be transmitted.

DATA SINK. The equipment which accepts data signals after transmission.

DELAY DISTORTION. The difference it takes, in time, for signals of different frequencies to pass through the phone line.

DEMODULATION. The process of retrieving an original signal from a modulated carrier wave. This technique is used in data sets to make communication signals compatible with business machine signals.

DIAL-UP. The use of a dial or push-button telephone to initiate a station-to-station telephone call.

DIRECT DISTANCE DIALING (D.D.D.). A telephone service which enables a user to dial directly telephones outside the user's local area without the aid of an operator.

DISK STORAGE. A storage device which uses magnetic recording on flat rotating disks.

DISTORTION, AMPLITUDE VS FREQUENCY. That distortion in a transmission system caused by the non-uniform attenuation or gain of the system with respect to frequency.

DISTORTION, DELAY VS FREQUENCY. That distortion in a transmission system caused by the difference between the maximum transit time and the minimum transit time of frequencies within a certain band under specified conditions. (Also called time delay distortion and non-linear phase distortion.)

DISTORTION, NON-LINEAR. Distortion caused by a deviation from a linear relationship between the input and output of a system or component.

DISTRIBUTED PROCESSING. A general term, usually referring to the use of intelligent or programmable terminals at sites remote from a company's main computer facility.

DROP. A connection made available for a terminal unit on a transmission line.

EBCDIC. (extended binary coded decimal interchange code) This 8-bit code is one of the two basic codes used in the IBM System. The other is an extended version of the USASCII code, called 8 bit USASCII (USASCII-8).

ECHO SUPPRESSOR. Used to attenuate echos on long telephone connections. The unit, inserted at four-wire points, functions by increasing the loss in the transmission path that is opposite in direction to the one being used. The hang-over time required for the echo suppressor to release, usually in the 15 to 100 millisecond range, depending on the type used. Generally it limits the speed with which data transmission can be turned around.

EIA INTERFACE. A standardized set of signal characteristics (time duration, voltage and current) specified by the Electronic Industries Association.

ERROR CONTROL. An arrangement that will detect the presence of errors. In some systems, refinements are added that will correct the detected errors, either by operations on the received data or by retransmission from the source.

ERROR BURST. A sudden outbreak of errors in a short amount of time compared to the period of errors immediately before and after the occurrence.

ERROR DETECTING CODE. A code in which each telegraph or data signal conforms to specific rules of construction so that departures from this construction in the received signals can be automatically detected. Such codes require more signal elements than are necessary to convey the fundamental information.

ERROR DETECTING SYSTEM. A system employing an error detecting code and so arranged that any signal detected as being in error is either deleted from the data delivered to the data sink, with or without an indication that such deletion has taken place, or delivered to the data sink together with an indication that it has been detected as being in error.

ERROR DETECTING AND FEEDBACK SYSTEM. (Decision feedback system, requests repeat system, ARQ system). A system employing an error detecting code and so arranged that a signal detected as being in error automatically initiates a request for retransmission of the signal detected as being in error.

ERROR RATE. The ratio of the number of bits, elements, characters or blocks incorrectly received to the total number of bits, elements, characters, or blocks transmitted.

EQUALIZATION. The process of reducing the effect(s) of amplitude frequency and/or phase distortion of a circuit by the introduction of networks to compensate for the difference in attenuation and/or time delay at the various frequencies in the transmission band.

EXCHANGE. A defined area, served by a communications common carrier, within which the carrier, furnishes service at the exchange rate and under the regulations applicable in that area as prescribed in the carrier's filed tariffs.

EYE PATTERN. An oscilloscope display that may be used to visually determine the quality of the equalized received line signal. An example would be the levels of an AM system, the opening being displayed on the scope in the shape of the human eye (as viewed full face; therefore the name "eye" pattern). In modern multilevel multiphase modems, it may be a series of dots that describe both in amplitude and phase, the location of various information levels.

FSK. Frequency Shift Keying. Most common form of frequency modulation in which two possible states (one and zero) are transmitted as two separate frequencies.

FACILITY. Communications equipment used, or available for use, in furnishing communications service.

FACSIMILE (FAX). A system of telecommunication for the transmission of images for reproduction on a permanent form. (Wire photo and tele-photo are facsimile through wire circuits; radio photo is facsimile via radio).

FEEDBACK. The return of part of the output of a machine, process, or system, to the computer as input from another phase especially for self-correcting or control purposes.

FLIP-FLOP. A circuit that is used to store one bit of information.

FOREIGN EXCHANGE. Connects a customer's service to a remote exchange. This service provides the equivalent of local service from the distant exchange.

FOUR-WIRE CHANNEL. A two-way circuit where signals follow separate and distinct paths in opposite directions in the transmission medium.

FREQUENCY DIVISION MULTIPLEX (FDM). A system of transmission in which characters or bits belonging to separate messages modulate a series of separate carriers transmitted simultaneously on a single circuit.

FULL DUPLEX. Refers to a communications system or equipment capable of transmission simultaneously in two directions.

HALF DUPLEX. A communication system capable of transmission alternately but not simultaneously in two directions.

HANDSHAKING. Exchange of predetermined signals for purposes of control when a connection is established between two data sets.

HARD COPY. A printed copy of machine output in readable form.

HERTZ. A unit of frequency equal to one cycle per second.

HOLDING TIME. The length of time a communication channel is in use for each transmission. Includes both message time and operating time.

HOME LOOP. An operation involving only those input and output units associated with the local terminal.

ICA. (integrated communications adapter) An integrated adapter that allows connection of multiple communication lines to a processing unit.

IMS. (information management system) A program product that uses OS (operating system) BTAM to allow IMS applications to operate on the remote terminal system. Remote display stations require non-switched lines.

INFORMATION BIT. One of those bits which are used to specify the characters of a given code group (opposed to framing bits).

INTERFACE. A shared boundary; for example, the physical connection between two systems or two devices.

INTERFACE EIA STANDARD RS-232 B OR C. A standardized method adopted by the Electronic Industries Association to insure uniformity of interface between data communication equipment and data processing terminal equipment. Has been generally accepted by most manufacturers of data transmission and business equipment.

INTERFACE—MIL STD 188B. The standard method of interface established by the Department of Defense. It is presently mandatory for use by the departments and agencies of the Department of Defense for the installation of all new equipment. This standard provides the interface requirements for connection between data communication security devices, data processing equipment, or other special military terminal devices.

INTERFACE—CCITT. The world recommendation for interface requirements between data processing terminal equipment and data communication equipment. The CCITT recommendation resembles very closely the American EIA Standard RS-232-B or C. This standard is considered mandatory in Europe and on the other continents.

LASER. A device which transmits an extremely narrow and coherent beam of electromagnetic energy in the visible light spectrum.

LEASED CHANNEL. A point-to-point channel reserved for sole use of a single leasing customer.

LINE HIT. An electrical interference causing the introduction of spurious signals on a circuit.

LINE SPEED. The maximum data rate that can be reliably transmitted over a line. Varies with capability of data set used.

LIST PROCESSING. A method of processing data in the form of lists.

LOCAL LOOP. That part of a communication circuit between the subscriber's equipment and the equipment in the phone company exchange (either 2-wire or 4-wire).

LONGITUDINAL REDUNDANCY CHECK (LRC). A system of error control based on the formation of a block check following preset rules. A check formation rule is applied in the same manner to each character.

MARK. One of the two possible conditions of an information element (bit); a closed line in a circuit.

MAGNETIC DRUM. A circular cylinder with a magnetic surface on which data can be stored by selective magnetization of portions of the curved surface.

MASER. Microwave Amplification by Stimulated Emission of Radiation—The general class of microwave amplifiers based on molecular interaction with electromagnetic radiation. The non-electronic nature of the Maser principle results in very low noise.

MEDIUM. (plural; media) The material on which data is recorded; for example, paper tape, cards, or magnetic tape.

MESSAGE FORMAT. Rules for the placement of such portions of a message as message heading, address, text and end of message.

MESSAGE NUMBERING. The identification of each message within a communication system by the assignment of a sequential number.

MESSAGE SWITCHING. The switching technique of receiving a message, storing it until the proper outgoing circuit and station are available, and then retransmitting it toward its destination.

MICROWAVE. All electromagnetic waves in the radio frequency spectrum above 890 megahertz.

MNEMONIC ADDRESS. A simple address code that has some easily remembered relationship to the name of the destination; e.g., LA for Los Angeles, ATL for Atlanta.

MODE. A method of operation, for example, line mode, home mode, local mode, communicate mode, etc.

MODEM. Acronym for modulator-demodulator.

MODULATION. The process of varying some characteristic of the carrier wave in accordance with the instantaneous value or samples of the intelligence to be transmitted.

MODULATION, AMPLITUDE (AM). Form of modulation in which the amplitude of the carrier is varied in accordance with the instantaneous value of the modulating signal.

MODULATION, DIFFERENTIAL. A type of modulation in which the choice of the significant condition for any signal element is dependent upon the choice for the previous signal element. Differential phase shift keying DPSK modulation is an example.

MODULATION, FREQUENCY (FM). A form of modulation in which the instantaneous frequency of a sine wave carrier is caused to depart from the carrier frequency by an amount proportional to the instantaneous value of the modulating signal.

MODULATION, PHASE (PM). Form of modulation in which the angle relative to the unmodulated carrier angle is varied in accordance with the instantaneous value of the amplitude of the modulating signal.

MODULATION, PULSE AMPLITUDE (PAM). The form of modulation in which the amplitude of the pulse carrier is varied in accordance with successive samples of the modulating signal.

MODULATION, PULSE CODE (PCM). The form of modulation in which the modulating signal is sampled and the sample quantized and coded so that each element of the information consists of different kinds and/or numbers of pulses and spaces.

MULTIPLEX. To interleave or simultaneously transmit two or more messages on a single channel.

MULTIPLEXING. The division of a transmission facility into two or more channels.

MULTIPOINT CIRCUIT. A circuit connecting 3 or more stations.

NAK. The negative acknowledge character (see ACK).

NETWORK. 1. A series of points connected by communications channels. 2. The switched telephone network is the network of telephone lines normally used for dialed telephone calls. 3. A private network is a network of communications channels confined to the use of one customer.

NOISE MEASUREMENT UNITS. The following units are used to express weighted and unweighted circuit noise. They include terms used in American and International practice—either DBA or DBRN. Weighted circuit noise power, in db., referred to 3.16 picowatts (−85 dbm) which is 0 dba. Use of F1A line or HA1 receiver weighting shall be indicated in parenthesis, as required. DBRN—(Describes above reference noise.) Weighted circuit noise power in db referred to 1.0 picowatt (−90 dbm) which is 0 dbrn. Use of 144 line, 144 receiver, or C message weighting, parenthesis, as required. With C message weighting, as 1 milliwatt, 1000 cps tone will read +90 dbrn, but the same power as white noise randomly distributed over a 3kc band (nominally 300 to 3300 cps) will read approximately +88.5 dbrn (rounded off to +88 dbrn, due to frequency weighting.) With 144 weighting, as 1 milliwatt, 1000 cps tone will also read +90 dbrn, but the same 3kc white noise power would read only +82 dbrn, due to the different frequency weighting.

NOISE WEIGHTING. In measurement of circuit noise, a filter is used with a specific amplitude frequency characteristic. It is designed to give numerical readings which approximate the amount of transmission impairment due to the noise, to an average listener, using a particular class of telephone subset. The noise weightings generally used were established by the agencies concerned with public telephone service and are based on characteristics of specific commercial telephone subsets, representing successive stages of technological development. The coding of commercial apparatus appears in the nomenclature of certain weightings. The same weighting nomenclature and units are used in the military versions as well as the commercial noise measuring sets. 144 Line Weighting—A noise weighting used in a noise measuring set to measure noise on a line that would be terminated by a subset with a number 144 receiver or a similar subset. Meter scale readings are in dbrn (144 line). F1A Line Weighting —A noise weighting used in a noise measuring set to measure noise on a line that would be terminated by a 302 type or similar, subset. The meter scale readings are in dba (F1A). HA1 Receiver Weighting—A noise weighting used in a noise measuring set to measure noise across the HA1 receiver of a 302 type, or similar, subset. The meter scale readings are in the dba (HA1). C-Message Weighting—A noise weighting used in a noise measuring set to measure noise on a line that would be terminated by a 500 type, or similar, subset. The meter scale readings are in dbrn (C-Message). Flat Weighting—A noise measuring set measuring amplitude frequency characteristics which are flat over a specified frequency range. The frequency range must be stated. Flat noise power may be expressed in dbrn (F1-F2) or in dbm (F1-F2). The terms "3kc flat weighting" and "15kc flat weighting" from 30 cps to the upper frequency indicated.

OFF-LINE. Pertaining to equipment or devices not under direct control of the central processing unit. May also be used to describe terminal equipment which is not connected to a transmission line.

ON-LINE. Pertaining to peripheral equipment or devices in direct communication with the central processing unit. May also describe terminal equipment connected to a transmission line.

ON-LINE SYSTEM. A system in which the input data enters the computer directly from the point of origin and/or in which output data is transmitted directly to the location where it is used.

OPERATING TIME. The time required for dialing the call, waiting for the connection to be established and coordinating the forthcoming transaction with the personnel or equipment at the receiving end.

PARITY CHECK. Addition of non-information bits to data, making the number of ones in a grouping of bits either always even or always odd. This permits detection of bit groupings which contain single errors. It may be applied to characters, blocks, or any convenient bit grouping.

PHASE JITTER. A type of unwanted random distortion which results in the intermittent shortening or lengthening of the signals.

POINT-TO-POINT TRANSMISSION. Transmission of data between two points.

POLAR KEYING. Form of telegraph signal in which circuit current flows one direction for marking, the other for spacing.

POLLING. A centrally controlled method of calling a number of points to permit them to transmit information.

PRIVATE LINE OR PRIVATE WIRE. A channel or circuit furnished a subscriber for his exclusive use. Also called leased line.

QTAM. (queued telecommunications access method) This access method provides the capabilities of BTAM plus the capability of queued messages on direct access storage devices. QTAM may be employed for data collection, message switching, and many other teleprocessing uses. Both BTAM and QTAM insulate the programmer from most of the details involved in programming an IBM 370 X or 270X and the attached terminal devices.

RJE. Remote job entry.

REAL TIME. 1. Pertaining to the actual time during which a physical process takes place. 2. Pertaining to the performance of a computation during a period short in comparison with the actual time that the related physical process takes place in order that results of the computations can be used in guiding the physical process.

REDUNDANCY. The portion of the total information contained in a message which can be eliminated without loss of essential information.

REMOTE STATION. Data terminal equipment for communication with a data processing system from a location that is distant in time or space.

REPEATER. A system component which reconstitutes signals into standard voltages, currents and timing.

RESPONSE TIME. The amount of time elapsed between generation of an inquiry at a data communications terminal and receipt of a response at that same terminal. Response time, thus defined includes: Transmission time to the computer. Processing time at the computer, including access time to obtain any file records needed to answer the inquiry, and transmission time back to the terminal.

SDLC. (synchronous datalink control). SDLC is a communications line discipline associated with the IBM system network architecture SNA and offers a number of advantages to users of data networks. SDLC is IBM's newest line discipline and initiates, controls, checks, and terminates information exchanges or communications lines. Designed for full duplex operation simultaneously sending and receiving data.

SELECTIVE CALLING. The ability of a transmitting station to specify which of several stations on the same line is to receive a message.

SERIAL TRANSMISSION. A method of information transfer in which the bits composing a character are sent sequentially. Contrast with parallel transmission.

SIGNALING IN BAND. Signaling which utilizes frequencies within the intelligence band of a channel.

SIGNALING OUT OF BAND. Signaling which utilizes frequencies outside the intelligence band. Also used to indicate the use of a portion of a channel bandwidth provided by the medium such as a carrier channel, but denied to the speech or intelligence path by filters. It results in a reduction of the effective available bandwidth.

SIMPLEX. Loosely, a communications system or equipment capable of transmission in one direction only.

SPACE. One of the two possible conditions of an information element (bit); an open line in a neutral circuit.

START ELEMENT. The first element of a character in certain serial transmissions, used to permit synchronization.

STATION. One of the input or output points on a communications system.

STOP ELEMENT. The last element of a character in certain serial transmissions, used to insure recognition of next start element.

STORE AND FORWARD. Applied to communication systems in which messages are received at intermediate routing points and recorded (stored). They are then retransmitted to a further routing point or to the ultimate recipient.

SUPERVISORY CONTROL. Characters or signals which automatically actuate equipment or indicators at a remote terminal.

SWITCHED TELEPHONE NETWORK. A network of telephone lines normally used for dialed telephone calls.

SYNCHRONOUS. Having a constant time interval between successive bits, characters, or events.

SYNCHRONOUS TRANSMISSION. Transmission in which the sending and receiving instruments are operating continuously at substantially the same frequency and may be maintained, by means of correction, in a desired phase relationship.

TCAM. (telecommunications access method) Telecommunications Access Method controls the transfer of messages between the application program and the remote terminals and provides the high level message control language. TCAM macro instructions can be used to construct a message control program that controls messages between remote stations and between remote stations and applications programs. TCAM can be tailored to applications requirements through selection of the appropriate macro instructions and operands.

TSO. (timesharing option) TSO is used for timeshare and utilizes a typewriter mode support. It is a request/response or conversational mode type of interaction between the system and the terminals. Many remote features of the terminal can be supported in user written TSO command processes and TSO application programs.

TTY. Teletypewriter equipment.

TWX. Western Union teleprinter exchange service with real time direct connection between subscribers.

TARIFF. The published rates and specifications for a specific unit of equipment, facility or type of service provided by a communication common carrier.

TELEPRINTER. Term used to refer to the equipment used in a printing telegraph system. A teletypewriter.

TELEPRINTER EXCHANGE SERVICE. A service provided by communication common carriers to connect teleprinters. Similar to regular telephone service, customers dial calls from station to station but communicate using teleprinter equipment rather than telephones. See Telex and TWX.

TELEPROCESSING. A form of information handling in which a data processing system uses communications facilities.

TELETYPE. Trademark of the Teletype Corporation. Usually refers to a series of different types of teleprinter equipment such as transmitters, tape punches, reperforators, page printers, utilized for communication systems.

TELEX. International network of teleprinter subscriber service; also a domestic Western Union network.

TELPAK. A service offered by telephone companies for the leasing of wide band channels between two or more points. Telpak channels can be leased in groups of 60 or 240 voice grade channels.

TERMINAL. 1. A point at which information can enter or leave a communication network. 2. An input/output device to receive or send source data in an environment associated with the job to be performed, capable of transmitting entries to and obtaining output from the system of which it is a part.

TEXT. That part of the message which contains the substantive information to be conveyed. Sometimes called "body" of the message.

THROUGHPUT. The total useful information processed or communicated during a specified time period.

TIE LINE. A private line communication channel of the type provided by communications common carriers for linking two or more points together.

TIME DIVISION MULTIPLEXER. A device which permits the simultaneous transmission of many independent channels of varying speeds into a single high speed data stream.

TIMESHARING. Participation in available computer time by multiple users, via terminals; pertaining to the interleaved use of the time of a device.

TOLL CENTER. A central office where channels and toll message circuits terminate.

TRUNK. A single circuit between two points, both of which are switching centers and/or individual distribution points.

TURNAROUND TIME. The actual time required to reverse the direction of transmission from send to receive or vice versa on a half-duplex circuit.

USASCII. (USA standard code for information interchange) The standard code, using a coded character set consisting of 7-bit coded characters (eight bits, including parity check), used for information interchange among data processing systems, communications systems and associated equipment. The USASCII set consists of control characters and graphic characters.

UNATTENDED OPERATION. The automatic features of a station's operation which permits the transmission and reception of messages on an unattended basis.

VNL. Via Net Loss—This term describes the net losses of trunks in the long distance switched telephone network of North America. The trunk is said to be in a via condition when it is an intermediate trunk in a longer switched connection.

VTAM. (virtual telecommunications access method) VTAM residing in an IBM system 370 is the access method or line which gives users at remote terminals access to applications programs. It also provides resource sharing, a technique for efficiently using a network to reduce transmission costs. For example, VTAM permits one terminal to share many application programs, eliminating the need to install a separate terminal and communication lines for each application.

VU. Volume Unit—The unit of measurement for electrical speech power in communication work as measured by a VU meter (volume indicator). Zero VU equals zero dbm in a measurement of sine wave test tone power.

VOICE GRADE CHANNEL. A channel suitable for transmission of speech, digital or analog data, or facsimile, generally with a frequency range of about 300 to 3000 cycles per second.

WATS. Wide Area Telephone Service—A service provided by telephone companies which permits a customer by use of an access line to make calls to telephones in a specific zone on a dial basis for a flat monthly charge, or to receive "collect" calls at a specified number at a flat monthly charge.

WPM. Words per minute.

WIDEBAND CHANNEL. A channel wider in bandwidth than a voice-grade channel.

references

Abrams, M.; Blanc, R.P.; and Cotton, I.W. *Computer Networks: A Tutorial.* New York: IEEE, 1975.

Abramson, N. "Packet switching with satellites." *Proceedings of the 1973 National Computer Conference,* AFIPS 42 (1973): 695–702.

Alusic, D.J. "Isochronous Communications—A Data Transmission Bridge." *Infosystems* (September 1975): 50–52.

Ashenhurst, R.L., and Vonderohe, R.H. "A Hierarchical Network." *Datamation* (February 1975): 40–44.

Bazovsky, I. *Reliability Theory and Practice.* Englewood Cliffs, N.J.: Prentice-Hall, Inc., 1961.

Becker, H.B. "Let's Put Information Networks into Perspective." *Datamation* (March 1978): 81–86.

Berglund, R.G. "Comparing Network Architectures." *Datamation* (February 1978): 79–85.

Blanc, R.P., and Cotton, I.W. *Computer Networking.* New York: IEEE Press, 1976.

Booth, G.M. "Distributed information Systems." *Proceedings of the 1976 National Computer Conference,* AFIPS 45: 789–794.

———. "Hierarchical Configurations for Distributed Processing." In *Distributed Processing Tutorial,* edited by Liebowitz and Carson. New York: IEEE, 1977, pp. 6–29 to 6–30.

———. "The Use of Distributed Data Bases in Information Networks," *Distributed Processing Tutorial,* edited by Liebowitz and Carson. New York: IEEE, 1977, pp. 8–7 to 8–12.

Bray, O.H. "Distributed Database Design Considerations." *Distributed Processing Tutorial,* edited by Liebowitz and Carson. New York: IEEE, 1977, pp. 8–13 to 8–19.

Breslin, J., and Tashenberg, C.B. *Distributed Processing Systems: End of the Mainframe Era?* New York: AMACOM, 1978.

Brown, F. "There ain't no free lunch." *Computer Decisions* (n.d.): 46–47.

Brown, J.M. "Distributed RJE terminals combine with central DP," *Data Communications* 6: 12 (December 1977): 67–72.

Busignies, H. "Communications Channels." *Scientific American* 227:3 (September 1972): 99–113.

Canaday, R.H.; Harrison, R.D.; Ivie, E.L.; Ryder, J.L.; and Wehr, L.A. "A Back-end Computer for Data Base Management." *Communications of the ACM* 17:10 (October 1974): 575–582.

Cerf, V.G., and Curran, A. "The Future of Computer Communications." *Datamation* (May 1977): 105–114.

Cerf, V.G., and Kahn, R.E. "A Protocol for Packet Network Intercommunication." In *Computer Networks: A Tutorial,* edited by Abrams, Blaus, and Connton. New York: IEEE, 1975, p. 4–27 to 4–38.

Champine, G.A. "Six Approaches to Distributed Data Bases." *Datamation* (May 1977): 69–72.

Chang, H. "Putting SDLC to Work at Bank of America." *Data Communications* 6:7 (July 1977): 45–50.

Combs, B. "TYMNET: A Distributed Network." *Datamation* (July 1973): 40–43.

Computer Networks: Trends and Applications. New York: IEEE, 1974.

Cooper, R.A., and Riviere, C. "Understanding reliability helps the user optimize network performance." *Data Communications* 6:1 (January 1977): 63–66.

Cotton, I.W. "Net results—Data processing versus data communications." *Computer Decisions* (November 1976): 22.

———. "Net results—Layering of protocols." *Computer Decisions* (August 1976): 14.

——— "Net results—Packet switched services." *Computer Decisions* (February 1977): 12.

———. "Net results—What is a network?" *Computer Decisions* (May 1976): 12.

Cuccio, A.B.J. "Microprocessor Utilization in Transaction Terminal Nets." In *Distributed Processing Tutorial,* edited by Liebowitz and Carson. New York: IEEE 1977, pp. 4-34 to 4-37.

Curtice, R.M. "Data Independence in Data Base Systems." *Datamation* (April 1975): 65–71.

———. "Integrity in Data Base Systems." *Datamation* (May 1977): 64–68.

Cypser, R.J. *Communications Architecture for Distributed Systems.* Reading, Mass.: Addison-Wesley Publishing Company, 1978.

Data Communications Primer. White Plains, N.Y.: IBM Corporation, Form C20–1668 (no date).

Davey, J.R. "Modems." In *Computer Networks: A Tutorial,* edited by Abrams, Blaus, and Cotton. New York: IEEE, 1975, pp. 3-21 to 3-29.

Dick, G.M. "The Lowly Modem." *Datamation* (March 1977): 69–73.

Distributed Systems Handbook. Maynard, Mass.: Digital Equipment Corporation, 1978.

Doll, D.R. "Multiplexing and Concentration." In *Computer Networks: A Tutorial,* edited by Abrams, Blaus, and Cotton. New York: IEEE, 1975, pp. 3-30 to 3-38.

———. "Relating to three kinds of distributed function." *Data Communications* 6: 3 (March 1977): 37–42.

———. "Telecommunications Turbulence and the Computer Network Evolution." In *Computer Networks: A Tutorial,* edited by Abrams, Blaus, and Cotton. New York: IEEE 1975, pp. 2-34 to 2-43.

Down, P.J., and Taylor, F.E. *Why Distributed Computing?* Manchester, England: NCC Publications, 1976.

Drucker, P.F. *The Concept of the Corporation.* New York: The New American Library, 1964.

Elovitz, H.S., and Heitmeyer, C.L. "What is a computer network?" In *Computer Networks: A Tutorial* edited by Abrams, Blaus, and Cotton. New York: IEEE, 1975, pp. 1-4 to 1-11.

Enslow, P.H., Jr. "What is a Distributed Data Processing System?" *Computer* 11: 1 (January 1978): 13–21.

Farber, D.J. "A Ring Network." *Datamation* (February 1975): 44–46.

Feidelman, L. "Distributed Computing—It's a Small World." *Infosystems* (April 1977): 50–54.

FitzGerald, J., and Eason, T.S. *Fundamentals of Data Communications.* New York: John Wiley and Sons, 1978.

Fraser, A.G. "A Virtual Channel Network." *Datamation* (February 1975): 51–56.

Granholm, J.W., "Alphanumeric Display Terminals," *Distributed Processing Tutorial,* (Liebowitz and Carson, editors) IEEE, New York, 1977, p. 4–18 to 4–30.

Gray, J.P. "Line Control Procedures." In *Computer Networks: A Tutorial,* edited by Abrams, Blanc, and Cotton. New York: IEEE, 1975, pp. 4-6 to 4-17.

Gray, J.P., and Blair, C.R. "IBM's Systems Network Architecture." *Datamation* (April 1975): 51–56.

Haback, D.H. "As terminal types multiply, so do problems of selection." *Data Communications* 7: 7 (July 1978): 53–61.

Hannan, J., and Fried, L. "Should you decentralize?" *Computer Decisions.* (February 1977): 40–42.

Heard, E.L. "Thinking about Database Costs." *Datamation* (October 1977): 24–31.

Hellerman, H. *Digital Computer System Principles,* 2d ed. New York: McGraw-Hill Book Company, 1973.

Hirsch, P. "SITA: Rating a Packet-Switched Network." *Datamation* (March 1974): 60–63.

Hobbs, L.C. "Terminals." In *Distributed Processing Tutorial,* edited by Liebowitz and Carson. New York: IEEE, 1977, pp. 4–6 to 4–16.

Hoxie, G.H., and Shea, D.M. "One Year Later—Ten Hot Buttons Facing Management." *Infosystems* (September 1977): 60–65.

Hoxie, G.H., and Shea, D.M. "Ten Hot Buttons Facing Management." *Infosystems* (August 1976): 28–33.

Huen, W.; Greene, P.; Hochsprung, R.; and El-Dessouki, O. "A Network Computer for Distributed Processing." In *Distributed Processing Tutorial,* edited by Liebowitz and Carson. New York: IEEE, 1977, pp. 6–31 to 6–35.

IBM Synchronous Data Link Control: General Information. White Plains, N.Y.: IBM Corporation, Form GA27–3093, 1975.

IBM System/360: Introduction to Teleprocessing. White Plains N.Y.: IBM Corporation, Form C30–2007, 1968.

Inose, H. "Communications Networks." *Scientific American* 227: 3 (September 1972): 117–128.

Introduction to Advanced Communications Function. White Plains, N.Y.: IBM Corporation, Form GC30–3033, 1976.

Introduction to Minicomputer Networks. Maynard, Mass.: Digital Equipment Corporation, 1974.

Jasper, D.P. "Principles of network design." In *Computer Networks: A Tutorial,* edited by Abrams, Blaus, and Cotton. New York: IEEE, 1975, pp. 2–13 to 2–17.

Jones, J.H. "Distributed processing—Age of the application analyst." *Infosystems* (June 1977): 62–64.

Kallis, S.A. "Networks and Distributed Processing." *Mini-Micro Systems* (March 1977): 32–40.

Katzan, H. *Computer Data Management and Data Base Technology.* New York: Van Nostrand Reinhold Company, 1975.

———. *Introduction to Computers and Data Processing.* New York: D. Van Nostrand Company, 1979.

Keet, E.E. "Distributed data processing—the key is software." *Data Communications* 6: 10 (October 1977): 55–61.

Kelley, N. "Bank of America Goes Distributive." *Infosystems* (March 1977): 46–48.

Kirkley, J.L. "Distributed Definitions." *Datamation* (May 1976): 55.

———. "Happiness Is Distributed Processing." *Datamation* (March 1978): 79.

Lechner, J.A. "Simplified Reliability Calculations for Complicated Systems." *IEEE Transactions on Systems Science and Cybernetics,* vol. SSC-1, no. 1, November, 1965.

Liebowitz, B.H., and Carson, J.H. *Distributed Processing Tutorial.* New York: IEEE, 1977.

Lurin, E.S., and Metz, E.I. "Get Ready for VANs." *Datamation* (July 1978): 103–108.

Lusa, J.M. "Alive and Well." *Infosystems* (November 1976): 35–38.

———. "The Wave of the Future?" *Infosystems* (September 1977): 43–46.

Lynch, A. "Distributed processing solves mainframe problems." *Data Communications* 5: 6 (November/December 1976): 17–22.

McFadyen, J.H. "Systems Network Architecture: An Overview." *IBM Systems Journal* 15: 1 (1976): 4–23.

Mandell, M. "Distributed Data Processing." *Computer Decisions* (July 1978): 25–28.

Marshall, J.C. "Distributed Processing on Wall Street." *Datamation* (July 1973): 44–46.

Mills, D.L. "Communication Software." In *Computer Networks: A Tutorial,* edited by Abrams, Blaus, and Cotton. New York: IEEE, 1975, pp. 4-18 to 4-26.

Moore, W.G. "Going Distributed." *Mini-Micro Systems* (March 1977): 41–48.

Moulton, P.D., and Sander, R.C. "Another Look at SNA." *Datamation* (March 1977): 74–82.

Murphy, D.E., and Kallis, S.A., Jr. *Introduction to Data Communication.* Maynard, Mass.: Digital Equipment Corporation, 1971.

Myers, C.A., ed. *The Impact of Computers on Management.* Cambridge, Mass.: The M.I.T. Press 1967.

Newport, C.B., and Ryzlak, J. "Communication Processors." In *Computer Networks: A Tutorial,* edited by Abrams, Blaus, and Cotton. New York: IEEE, 1975, pp. 3-38 to 3-49.

Owen, S. "A Data Communications Primer." *Infosystems* (March 1977): 38.

Patrick, R.L. "Decentralizing Hardware and Dispersing Responsibility." *Datamation* (May 1976): 79–84.

Piatowski, T.F.; Hull, D.C.; and Sundstrom, R.J. "Inside IBM's Systems Network Architecture." *Data Communications* 6: 2 (February 1977): 33–48.

Pyke, T.N., Jr.; and Blanc, R.P. "Computer networking technology—a state of the art review." In *Computer Networks: A Tutorial,* edited by Abrams, Blaus, and Cotton. New York: IEEE, 1975, pp. 2-6 to 2-12.

Raymond, J., and Banerki, D.K. "Using a Microprocessor in an Intelligent Graphic Terminal." In *Distributed Processing Tutorial,* edited by Liebowitz and Carson. New York: IEEE, 1977, pp. 4-38 to 4-44.

Reynolds, C.H. "Issues in Centralization." *Datamation* (March 1977): 91–100.

Ritchie, R.O. "Evaluating Modems." *Datamation* (October 1974): 48–53.

Sanders, D.H. *Computers and Management.* New York: McGraw-Hill Book Company, 1974.

Sanders, R.W. "Comparing Networking Technologies." *Datamation* (July 1978): 88–93.

———. "Networking: An Overview." *Datamation* (March 1974): 54–55.

Saslow, S.M. "The 'Smart' Terminal." In *Distributed Processing Tutorial,* edited by Liebowitz and Carson. New York: IEEE, 1977, pp. 4-31 to 4-33.

Saxton, W.A., and Edwards, M. "Distributed processing revisited." *Infosystems* (July 1978): 108–109.

Schumacher, E.F. *Small Is Beautiful: Economics as if People Mattered.* New York: Harper and Row Publishers, 1973.

Sher, M.S. "A Case Study in Networking." *Datamation* (March 1974): 56–69.

Sherry's Guide to Data Communications Buzzwords. Miami, Fla.: Racal-Milgo Information Systems, Inc., 1978.

Simmons, D.B. "Texas A & M: University Network Serving Outside Users." *Datamation* (March 1974): 64–66.

Speers, G.S. "Monitoring/Control by Distributed Computing." *Datamation* (July 1973): 47–49.

Stein, P. "Distributed processing and reality." *Computer Decisions* (August 1976): 12.

Stiefel, M.L. "What is an 'Intelligent' Terminal?" In *Distributed Processing*

Tutorial, edited by Liebowitz and Carson. New York: IEEE, 1977, pp. 4-52 to 4-59.

Systems Network Architecture: General Information. White Plains, N.Y.: IBM Corporation, Form number GA27–3102, 1975.

Tenkhoff, P.A., and Collard, J.C. "The Common Carriers' Uncommon Offerings." *Datamation* (April 1975): 44–47.

Uhlig, R.P. "Human Factors in Computer Message Systems." *Datamation* (May 1977): 120–126.

Wetmore, S. "Abbreviations and acronyms in data communications." *Data Communications* 6: 11 (November 1977): 69–78.

White, W., and Holmes, M. "The Future of Commercial Satellite Telecommunications." *Datamation* (July 1978): 94–102.

Wulf, W., and Levin, R. "A Local Network." *Datamation* (February 1975): 47–50.

Zatyko, D. "Networking Can Distribute the Power of the Computer." *Infosystems* (March 1977): 39.

Zemrowski, K.M. "Problems of Data Base Use in a Distributed Data Network." In *Distributed Processing Tutorial*, edited by Liebowitz and Carson. New York: IEEE, 1977, pp. 8-20 to 8-27.

index